T3-BOR-515

WHAT TO EXPECT NOW
THAT YOU BELIEVE

BY
TOM ALLEN

CHRISTIAN PUBLICATIONS, INC.
CAMP HILL, PENNSYLVANIA

This book is dedicated to my brother Tim
who models Philippians 2:3 in his daily life:

"Do nothing out of selfish ambition
or vain conceit, but in humility consider
others better than yourselves." *(emphasis added)*

Christian Publications, Inc.
3825 Hartzdale Drive, Camp Hill, PA 17011
www.cpi-horizon.com
www.christianpublications.com

Faithful, biblical publishing since 1883

ISBN: 0-87509-774-X
© 2000 by Christian Publications, Inc.
All rights reserved
Printed in the United States of America

00 01 02 03 04   5 4 3 2 1

Table of Contents

FOREWORD

I have known Rev. Tom Allen for many years. He comes from a gifted family in the ministry that is widely known throughout The Christian and Missionary Alliance. Tom is devoted to his wife and children. He graduated from Asbury College in Wilmore, Kentucky, and from the Alliance Theological Seminary in Nyack, New York.

He has pastored Alliance churches, but for most of his life he has felt the call to itinerant evangelistic ministry. He has been very busy as a National Minister of Outreach both in the United States and abroad. His anointed preaching of the Word of God is balanced with social concern—a balance I firmly believe more evangelists need today.

Tom Allen is the author of a number of books. His latest—*What to Expect Now That You Believe*—could well be the best of all that he has written, and it is a *must read* for every believer. This one-of-a-kind resource represents a biblical basis for what the victorious Christian life is, and how to live that life in today's secularized, corrupt world. I highly recommend this fine book to everyone.

Dr. Howard O. Jones, Associate Evangelist
The Billy Graham Evangelistic Association

Great Expectations

When my first daughter, Andrea, was born, I rushed to the telephone to share the good news with my parents. I was so excited that I blurted out, "Oh, Mom and Dad, she's just perfect—five fingers and five toes!"

"Wait a minute, Tom," Dad interrupted. "Don't you mean ten fingers and ten toes?" They never let me forget that one!

Many interesting stories can be told surrounding the physical birth of a baby. The same is true for those who have recently experienced spiritual birth—those who have been "born again." If you fall into that category, I rejoice as I say to you, "Welcome to the family of God." It is always fascinating to hear how people came to faith in Jesus Christ. The Lord uses a wide variety of ways and

1

means to reach us with His grace, and no two testimonies of conversion are exactly alike.

Consider the contrast between my salvation story and that of my dad's.

My father, the late Bill Allen, had a very dramatic conversion experience. During his college years, he had embraced atheism—not so much because it was the best answer to his questions, but because it matched his materialistic mind-set. He wanted to live the lifestyle of the rich and famous, and at the age of twenty-two, he was well on his way. It was 1941, and Bill was the leading salesman for a life insurance company in Dayton, Ohio. On one particularly good day, he sold thirteen complete policies, with one man signing the documents while seated in the bathtub! At least my father could not have been accused of "dirty" sales tactics!

His godly mother-in-law could see the handwriting on the wall for her daughter and son-in-law. Apart from a radical conversion, it wouldn't be a pretty picture. She could envision the emptiness of a marriage focused on money. So she prayed. Mother Wills invited Bill to attend some special evangelistic meetings at her church. He declined. She persisted. Finally, he said, "OK, I'll go. But here's the stipulation. I will attend the service if you promise to never ask me to go again." She agreed to his condition. But that night, he listened to an evangelist who really believed what he was saying.

Bill had a flashback to his college days. Along with some friends from a psychology class, he had observed a "revival" meeting in a church to "psychoanalyze" the religious freaks in attendance. They had enjoyed a wonderful evening of mockery and mayhem. But this recent experience was entirely different. The speaker preached with real authority. My father was so intrigued that he decided to meet with the evangelist the next day. He would ask him some of his tried and true questions about the existence of God.

The atheist and the evangelist met for several hours. My father asked every question he could think of, and the answers he received made a lot of sense. At the end of their conversation, Bill Allen made this promise to himself: He would either return to the service that night and give his heart to Jesus Christ, or he would burn every Bible in the house and never talk about religion again. All or nothing. If Christ was the Savior He claimed to be, nothing less than full surrender made sense. And if Jesus was not who He claimed to be, utter rejection was the only recourse.

How grateful I am that my dad decided to return to the church that night. On the very last verse of the invitation hymn, a very proud, self-assured salesman humbled himself and invited Christ to become his Savior and Lord. Bill Allen became a new man. He instantly lost his taste for cigarettes and alcohol. He wanted to tell everyone about his faith. When he told his parents, Earl and Cynthia, about being "saved," his mother inquired, "Were you in an automobile accident, Bill?" Through much patience and persevering prayer, my grandparents came to Christ seven years later. It was not long before my father's desire to offer "eternal life insurance" superseded his passion to sell the earthly brand. He spent the next fifty years as a pastor and evangelist before God called him home in 1992.

My conversion experience was quite different in many respects. As a P.K. (preacher's kid), I grew up in an atmosphere of Christianity. I had heard the gospel from my first days in the church nursery. I knew the great hymns by heart. I memorized Scripture for Sunday school and vacation Bible school. But it was in a dream that I discovered my need for Christ to be my personal Savior.

I was eleven years old at the time. Our home on Brinkerhoff Avenue in Mansfield, Ohio, had a backyard that was divided down the middle with a stone walkway. In the dream, I was walking on the stones, and the area to my right represented heaven. To the left represented hell. My mom, my dad, my brothers and sisters all stood on that right side, and a voice asked a simple question: "Which side do you belong on, Tom?" In the dream, I had no definite answer. I woke up troubled. Certainly the son of the great minister, Rev. Bill Allen, should belong in heaven with the rest of his family. But why? On what basis?

Shortly after that dream, I accepted Christ as my personal Savior while attending a family camp in Toccoa Falls, Georgia. My father was the speaker. As I listened, it became clear to me that I wanted and needed Jesus to be my Lord and Savior. I was grateful for Christian parents, and also for brothers and sisters who had joined God's family. But that accomplished nothing for me. I could not get to heaven while hanging on to my parents' spiritual bootstraps. I needed to confess my sins and receive a new heart from the Holy Spirit, just like everyone else who is born again.

Obviously, I was not living a particularly "evil" life at the ripe old age of eleven. But I desperately needed to do what we all must do when we come to Christ for salvation: I had to give up the right to run my own life. Jesus took the steering wheel as I crawled into the backseat. His dreams would become my dreams, and His plans, my plans. It was a whole new view of Who would be in charge of Tom Allen's life. In this sense, my conversion experience was every bit as radical and revolutionary as my father's.

Gather ten Christians in a room to share their testimony, and you will hear ten unique accounts of amazing grace. But one common thread weaves its way through each testimony. All of us have great expectations for what our newfound faith will do in us, for us and through us. And there is justification for this optimism, according to well-known Scriptures:

> Therefore, if anyone is in Christ, he is a new creation; the old has gone, the new has come! (2 Corinthians 5:17)

> I have come that they may have life, and have it to the full. (John 10:10b)

These verses, along with many others, give all of us high hopes for an exciting future in our newfound faith. As I write this, I am entering my thirty-fourth year as a believer. I can testify to the fact that life has indeed been "to the full" in Christ. There have been joys and blessings too numerous to count. But I must honestly balance this reality with the fact that there have also been many setbacks, burdens and trials along the way. At times, "great expectations" turned into "great disappointments."

This book is an attempt to balance those great expectations that every new believer embraces when he or she first joins the family of God. Hopefully, it will serve as a "reality check." The question, "What should I expect when I become a Christian?" is a big one. The answer will have many layers.

THREE STAGES OF CHRISTIAN EXPERIENCE

I have three stages of Christian experience in mind as I write this. First, those who have become believers within the past twelve months. Second, those who have been Christians from two to five years. And third, people who have walked with Christ for six or more years.

The first group may be so new in the faith that the middle chapters of this book will seem strange or even offensive. You will be tempted to resist this truth. Please bear with me. Take it by faith. Time and experience in your walk with the Lord will prove the truth of those pages.

That second group—those who have been Christians for a few years—will probably be relieved by what they discover here. Having been beaten up a little in the battle, these believers will be pleased to know that they are not alone. In fact, trials, temptation, persecution and doubts are part and parcel of "what to expect" as a Christian.

And I hope that those who have been walking the path for several years will be refreshed by the reminders in these pages. It is easy to forget what Jesus said regarding both the pleasures and the pressures of the faith. We are prone to take certain things for granted as the years pass by. It is healthy for us to periodically be refreshed with regard to who we are in Christ, what to expect in our walk with Him and how He has provided for our every need.

We should never abandon our "great expectations" as believers. The greatest of them all may take place very soon when Christ returns and we receive our glorified bodies. But while we await "the sweet by-and-by," we need to learn how to cope with "the nasty here-and-now." The challenge of writing this book for me is to balance great expectations with realistic expectations. To the degree that this is accomplished and believers are encouraged, I give God the glory.

Tom Allen
January, 2000

CHAPTER 1

Expect Forgiveness

The story is told of a wealthy Chicago man who had two sons. Because of his incredible success as a businessman, he was able to put away ten million dollars in a trust fund for his boys when they were just eight and ten years old. This was to be divided equally among them when they turned twenty-one years of age.

As they grew older, these two sons began to demonstrate just how very different they were. The older one, Steve, was disciplined, punctual and dependable in every way. The younger boy, Jack, was unorganized, fickle and routinely late for every appointment. One could only wonder how these two young men could even be related!

The summer before Steve's senior year in college, Jack, now twenty-one and about to enter his sophomore year, decided to drop out of school. With five million dollars just waiting for him to spend, it was difficult to focus on his studies. So against the wishes of his parents, Jack left school, left home and began to spend his trust fund with reckless abandon.

First came the Mercedes. Then the BMW. A few months later, a Lexus. Jack started gambling. He dabbled in real estate. He experimented with alcohol and drugs. Warning after warning came from his financial advisor, but Jack ignored them. The money was disappearing faster than a snowball in Miami. But he was having too much fun living it up with the proceeds from the trust fund.

While Jack was blowing cash big time, his older brother Steve had graduated from college, married his high school sweetheart and taken the position of vice-president in his father's corporation. He could only watch his little brother's rapid self-destruction from a distance, and it was not a pretty sight. "Steady Steve" stayed near home, helped to secure the family fortune and tried to please his father in every way.

Within three years, Jack had, through unwise and undisciplined management, reduced his net worth to a few thousand dollars. He was working by order of the court on a farm owned by a Mr. Jones. He had crashed his last new car into Jones' barn destroying some very expensive farm equipment. Jack was driving under the influence at the time. As he was slopping the hogs one day, he found himself reaching for a half-eaten apple that had been discarded for pig food. In a flash, one of the pigs snatched it away and pinched Jack in the process.

That's when it really hit him.

"Mom and Dad are back in Chicago with maids and servants waiting on them. My brother Steve has a wife, a great job and a secure future. And look what I've got! I've squandered my trust fund to zilch, I've had to forfeit my cars and properties, and I'm sitting here fighting with a pudgy pig for half of an apple! This is absurd! I'm going back to Illinois. I'm going to make things right with my parents, and ask for a job—whatever they could offer me would be better than this! Life at home was much better than I thought." So he purchased an old beat-up car with the last of his money and headed for Chicago.

Jack's father took his daily walk down the long, winding driveway leading to his estate. Every day, he prayed that his son would return to his senses, come home and begin to live a productive life. Then he saw him. The dented, rusty vehicle slowly made its way in his direction. Billows of smoke followed the automobile. The father began to run as fast as he could. He was waving his arms wildly as he approached Jack's car.

As his son staggered out of the driver's seat, the father hugged him and kissed him before he could even say a word. Jack was stunned at this open display of affection in the light of his enormous failure. Many tears were shed as they embraced. Finally Jack was able to blurt out his heartfelt confession: "Dad, I blew it big-time. I have disgraced both God and our family with my sin. Frankly, I don't even deserve to be called by the same last name. Could you ever forgive me? I'll gladly take the lowest paying job you have to offer."

By this time, some of the servants had arrived at the scene on the driveway. They could hardly believe that this was Jack and that he had returned home. After assuring his son of his complete forgiveness, the father began to fire off orders to the servants: "Get to the meat market and buy the best filet mignon steak. Then go to the store and get all the trimmings for a "Welcome Home!" party. Tonight will be a very special night in this house. My son, whom I had given up for dead is alive again. He was lost, and now we found him."

When word got to Steve at the office that his profligate brother had finally returned home, he was repulsed at the very notion. And when he got the invitation to attend the gala event that evening, he began to question his father's sanity! He quickly phoned his dad in protest: "Have you lost your mind? I have faithfully served you in the family business all these years while Jack has been goofing around, blowing his inheritance. I can't ever remember you throwing a party for me and my friends! But when Jack comes back, you roll out the red carpet—what's up with that?"

The father gently replied, "Steve, I am grateful for the fact that I have been able to count on you. Your faithfulness means a lot to me. But your long-lost brother Jack was like a dead man who suddenly came back to life. We lost him for awhile, but now we found him. This is worth celebrating in a big way!"

If this story sounds familiar, it's because I have taken it right out of the Bible. It's a modernized version of the parable of the lost son in Luke 15:11-32. This is perhaps the most dramatic way our Lord could say it. When we turn to Him we can expect forgiveness.

FORGIVENESS DEFINED

The Greek word for "forgiveness" is *aphesis*. In classical Greek, it was a judicial term that referred to the "release from a legal relationship." This was used in the context of being emancipated from a debt, for instance, or a marriage. The usage of *aphesis* in the New Testament carries nuances of freedom from the debt of sin. Deliverance from the domination of iniquity. Pardon from past sins as in a prisoner whose sentence was revoked. This is the glorious liberty of the sons and daughters of God. This is the freedom that the lost son experienced when he came home to the father in Luke 15.

So, just what kind of forgiveness can we expect? Consider with me several characteristics which emanate from this parable.

UNEXPECTED

The lost son, or "Jack," as we've come to know him, in no way expected to be forgiven so completely and immediately. He was nonplused by his father's reaction. He had anticipated some kind of punishment, and perhaps even banishment for a period of time. Jack was assuming that he would have to beg his way back into the good graces of his family. The enormity of his sin was too overwhelming to be so easily resolved. But the unexpected happened: he was forgiven for his transgressions, and his status as a son was immediately reaffirmed.

One very notable detail in this story is often overlooked: the hug and kiss took place before the son could utter one word of confession! Here's how it reads: "But while he was still a long way off, his father saw him and was filled with compassion for him; he ran to his son, threw his arms around him and kissed him" (Luke 15:20).

We would have expected that the father would have waited to see just how contrite this boy was before he allowed himself to become emotional.

Not so. The father made the first move by running out to meet the son. The father offered his affection and compassion before a word was spoken. So it is with the unexpected love of God when we come home to Him.

There are many illustrations of people who were caught off guard by the unexpected forgiveness offered by Jesus Christ. Zacchaeus was so shocked that he instantly gave up half of his estate to the poor, and then committed to make restitution at the astronomical rate of 400 percent (19:1-10). A prostitute responded to this pardon for sin by washing the feet of Jesus with her tears, and then kissing those feet and pouring expensive perfume on them (7:36-50).

It is understandable that our forgiveness is unanticipated. Deep within every human heart is the sense that we have sinned—we have "missed the mark" of God's high standard. Along with that, we have this nagging suspicion that someone has to pay for this. Our initial thought is to try to take care of the bill personally. But then we finally discover that the sinless Son of God made that payment once-and-for-all with His very own life. It was a debt we could have never repaid. This is both stunning and wonderful. Paul describes it this way:

> This righteousness from God comes through faith in Jesus Christ to all who be-

lieve. There is no difference, for all have
sinned and fall short of the glory of God,
and are justified freely by his grace through
the redemption that came by Christ Jesus.
God presented him as a sacrifice of atone-
ment, through faith in his blood. . . .
(Romans 3:22-25)

In him we have redemption through his
blood, the forgiveness of sins, in accordance
with the riches of God's grace that he lav-
ished on us. . . . (Ephesians 1:7-8)

C.S. Lewis makes an interesting observation
about Christianity being real because of this ele-
ment of the unexpected:

Reality, in fact, is usually something you
could not have guessed. That is one of the reasons I believe Christianity. It is a religion you
could not have guessed. If it offered us just the
kind of universe we had always expected, I
should feel we were making it up. But, in fact,
it is not the sort of thing anyone would have
made up. It has just that queer twist about it
that real things have.[1]

To say "expect forgiveness" is really the same as
saying "expect the unexpected." We can only "expect" it because pardon has been freely offered to

us at a high cost to Christ. We should not "expect" it in the sense of "taking it for granted." This leads to our next consideration.

UNDESERVED

Look at the heartfelt statement made by the lost son when he returned to his father's embrace: "Father, I have sinned against heaven and against you. I am no longer worthy to be called your son" (Luke 15:21).

This young man knew what he deserved. The father would have been more than justified by simply agreeing with his son and leaving it at that:

> "You know something, Jack? You are absolutely correct. You have shamed this family so deeply we may never recover from it. Your mother has been worried sick about you. Your brother doesn't even want to hear your name spoken around the house. I suggest you go to the courthouse tomorrow and change your name. If you show sufficient evidence of repentance after a period of probation, we will give consideration to offering the family name back to you. But for now, let's not think of you as a part of this family."

In the same way, we do not "deserve" to be members of God's family. The forgiveness that led to our spiritual adoption was not something that we had coming to us. On the contrary, our many sins made us candidates for judgment. How we can thank God that "he does not treat us as our sins deserve or repay us according to our iniquities" (Psalm 103:10).

UNEARNED

Jack knew that he had not earned the "Welcome Home" party that was given in his honor that night. He was acutely aware of the fact that he did nothing to merit his return to the full rights of a son. It would have been impossible for him to earn enough money to repay the inheritance that he so quickly disposed of during his days of wild living. And that was precisely the point which our Lord was making through this parable. Our forgiveness cannot be earned—it must be granted.

The apostle Paul clarified this for us: "For it is by grace you have been saved, through faith—and this not from yourselves, it is the gift of God—not by works, so that no one can boast" (Ephesians 2:8-9).

I'll never forget the testimony of a young couple in a church I pastored. Their little boy was enrolled in our Bible club program. One day, as they were going over memory verses with their son, he recited Ephesians 2:8-9. As the parents checked the Bible to see that he was repeating the words correctly, the truth suddenly flooded into their souls. Not long after that, both mom and dad gave their hearts to Christ.

Before I baptized this couple, they shared this story with me. They had been a part of a church that taught them to make every attempt to work their way to heaven. As these verses from Ephesians jumped out that day, they realized that Jesus had provided salvation as a gift. They could never earn it even with a lifetime of good works.

This is why the prophet Isaiah declares that "all our righteous acts are like filthy rags" (Isaiah 64:6).

This is a rather blunt way of saying that our good deeds are useless. Why? Because even when combined over decades, our self-righteousness would never be good enough to satisfy the demands of a holy God. Only one person has ever lived a life that completely fulfilled those stringent requirements. His name is Jesus Christ. And only His sacrifice on the cross was adequate to cleanse our hearts and make us presentable to His Father. The Savior earned our place in God's family in a way that no one else could.

Chuck Colson visited a prison near the city of Sao José dos Campos, Brazil. The Brazilian government had turned the operation of this facility over to two Christians some twenty years earlier. The institution was renamed Humaita. For two decades it has been run on Christian principles. Mr. Colson visited the prison and made this report:

> When I visited Humaita I found the inmates smiling—particularly the murderer who held the keys, opened the gates and let me in. Wherever I walked I saw men at peace. I saw clean living areas, people working industriously. The walls were decorated with biblical sayings from Psalms and Proverbs. . . . My guide escorted me to the notorious prison cell once used for torture. Today, he told me, that block houses only a single inmate. As we reached the end of a long concrete corridor and he put the key in the lock, he paused and asked, "Are you sure you want to go in?"
>
> "Of course," I replied impatiently, "I've been in isolation cells all over the world."
>
> Slowly he swung open the massive door, and I saw the prisoner in that punishment cell: a crucifix, beautifully carved by the Humaita inmates—the prisoner Jesus, hanging on a cross.

"He's doing time for the rest of us," my guide said softly.[2]

 UNLIMITED

The story in Luke 15 would seem very different if the father had said this to his son upon his return:

> "Thanks for the confession, Jack, and I'm really glad to see that you are sorry for all your foolishness. But there are limitations in my ability to forgive you. I can excuse you for your sexual immorality and drunkenness. But it will take me a long time to forgive you for wasting that five million dollar inheritance that I worked so hard to provide. I'm not sure that I will ever be able to grant a pardon for that."

Thankfully, the story is quite clear on this point. The forgiveness extended to the lost son was unlimited with no strings attached. The father never implied that his son would be exonerated "to a certain extent." It was a full pardon. John tells us about the complete nature of our forgiveness: "If we confess our sins, he is faithful and just and will forgive us our sins and purify us from all unrighteousness" (1 John 1:9).

The prophet Micah celebrated unlimited forgiveness in this way:

> Who is a God like you,
>   who pardons sin and forgives the
>   transgression
>   of the remnant of his inheritance?
> You do not stay angry forever
>   but delight to show mercy.
> You will again have compassion on us;
>   you will tread our sins underfoot
>   and hurl all our iniquities into the
>   depths of the sea. (Micah 7:18-19)

The key word in both of these texts is *all*—*all* unrighteousness, *all* our iniquities. Because Jesus paid it all, every sin imaginable has been covered by His shed blood. The writer of Hebrews states it this way: ". . . we have been made holy through the sacrifice of the body of Jesus Christ once for all" (Hebrews 10:10).

This seems impossible when we first see it. Could it be that even a man like Adolph Hitler could be completely forgiven if he had confessed his sins in his dying moments and trusted Christ as his Savior? Yes, it could be. The reason is both simple and profound. Hitler's forgiveness would not have been based on the number or the nature of his sins. The pardon would have been granted on the basis of the power of the blood of Jesus

Christ. And that power is greater than anyone's pile of iniquity, regardless of how high it is stacked or how much it stinks.

What incredibly good news this is for the "repeat offenders" among us—perhaps 99.9 percent of us (including me!). No one can ever say, "I've committed too many sins to be a candidate for Christ's forgiveness," or "I've repeated the same sin so many times that I am beyond His pardon." We are dealing with a Savior who is absolutely unlimited in both His ability and willingness to forgive.

Philip P. Bliss captured the glory of this truth in his classic hymn, "It Is Well with My Soul":

> My sin—oh, the bliss of this glorious
>   thought—
> My sin, not in part but the whole,
> Is nailed to His cross and I bear it no more!
> Praise the Lord, praise the Lord, O my soul![3]

Unexpected, undeserved, unearned and unlimited—this is the kind of forgiveness we can expect now that we have become Christians. What gratitude this inspires! What hope this instills! Is there not an appropriate response we could make in the light of the mercy shown to us in the amazing forgiveness of Christ? I'm glad you asked. One other quality of forgiveness should be examined.

UNLEASHED

Jesus and Paul made challenging statements about our need to forgive others: "For if you forgive men when they sin against you, your heavenly Father will also forgive you. But if you do not forgive men their sins, your Father will not forgive your sins" (Matthew 6:14-15). "Forgive as the Lord forgave you" (Colossians 3:13).

These verses tell us that the spirit of forgiveness toward those who have wounded us should be unleashed inside our hearts because of this profound reality: we have been forgiven by God for our many sins. Without this forgiving heart toward others, we are no longer eligible for the Lord's pardon in our own lives. Actually, it is a very simple matter. Forgiven people forgive. Those who find it difficult to cancel someone else's debt never really understood the depth of their own bankruptcy before God.

In the story of the lost son, the older brother, "Steve," seems to have a very difficult time with this concept of forgiveness. His reaction went something like this:

> "Dad, think about what you're doing here. I am your 'good son.' I've been faithful and obedient for a number of years. I would have loved to have had parties with my

friends, even if it was just hamburgers on the grill. Now Jack comes back bankrupt after years of immorality and drunkenness, and you bring out the filet mignon! How could you possibly forgive him so quickly and completely? None of this makes any sense at all!" (Luke 15:29-30, author's paraphrase).

Our natural instinct would be to applaud this older brother. We can understand his bitter reaction to the full pardon of his sinful sibling. Something inside each of us wants to see a playboy like this "pay his dues." We don't want Jack to be forgiven instantly and utterly. "There should be some consequences," we say, with more than just a twinge of self-righteousness.

The truth is that Jack did have to face some consequences for his actions. He may have had a sexually transmitted disease to cope with as a result of his immorality. Jack had squandered his huge inheritance. It would take a lifetime to get that back. He would have many painful memories to work through. But the most important reality of all was this: Jack was a forgiven man!

Though we have no record to specifically confirm this, we can assume that the older brother had not lived a totally perfect life there in his hometown. Perhaps his sins had not been as public or blatant, but he, too, was a candidate for forgive-ness. He, too, had missed the mark of God's stan-dard.

Perhaps Steve's greatest iniquity was his pride. He was quite impressed with himself, and his steady, faithful commitment to his father and the family. His attitude is very reminiscent of the Pharisee in Luke 18: "God, I thank you that I am not like other men—robbers, evildoers, adulterers. . . . I fast twice a week and give a tenth of all I get" (Luke 18:11,12).

Jack's demeanor, in stark contrast, was like the tax collector in that same parable: "God, have mercy on me, a sinner" (18:13).

Steve was an arrogant sinner who didn't even know he needed forgiveness. Therefore he couldn't forgive Jack, and he could not be forgiven by God in that state of mind. But Jack was a humbled sinner who knew that he desperately needed forgiveness. Therefore he was forgiven, and he could forgive oth-ers—even his older brother and his bitter heart. Atti-tude is everything: "This is the one I esteem: he who is humble and contrite in spirit, and trembles at my word" (Isaiah 66:2).

Let me be quick to point out that forgiving others is easier to understand as a principle than it is to un-dertake as a practice in real life. I have counseled young people who were sexually abused by a parent. They describe an ongoing struggle with hatred and rancor toward the offending adult. Left only to human power and virtue, this would be a hopeless scenario. But the same Jesus who provided our forgiveness can place that spirit of pardon within our hearts—even for the most severe transgressions. Even as Paul said that "Christ lives in me" (Galatians 2:20), it can be "Christ forgives through me."

So we should expect forgiveness from God even though it is unexpected, unearned, unlimited and undeserved. And we should also expect that the reality of our forgiven status will be unleashed in the form of pardon for those who offend us. This is what to expect now that you believe.

ENDNOTES

[1] C.S. Lewis, *Mere Christianity* (New York: Macmillan, 1960), p. 33.

[2] Charles Colson, "Making the World Safe for Religion," *Christianity Today*, November 8, 1993, p. 33.

[3] Philip P. Bliss, "It Is Well with My Soul," *Hymns of the Christian Life* (Camp Hill, PA: Christian Publications, 1978), # 300.

CHAPTER 2

Expect Joy

*H*e was handicapped as the result of a birth defect. Crippled from birth, Patrick had never known the freedom of being able to walk or run. His family was unable to pay for his health insurance. Bills from various doctors and hospitals were stacking up. They did the only thing they could think of doing: they took Patrick out to beg for money. Certainly people would have compassion on him if they could just see his plight.

His parents wondered where to place their son so that he could earn the most money. They thought about busy street corners in New York City. Perhaps a shopping mall. No, there would be laws against that. Then it came to them: Why not place Patrick outside a large church or temple along a main thoroughfare? Religious people would be the most likely to have compassion on their crippled son. And others might join the cause if they saw the churchgoers helping him. And just maybe a minister would come along and pray for the boy.

Before long, they selected what appeared to be the ideal location. It was a large temple with a grand archway covered in shimmering brass. It was situated in a high-traffic area in the heart of the city. Each and every day, Patrick was laid at the doorway to the temple. Propped up against his side was a sign that read: "Crippled since birth. Cannot afford health insurance. Any assistance most appreciated."

And so he held his plate out to all who passed by in the hopes that some would contribute to his cause. Many did help. But others, even some of the ministers, ignored the crippled young man.

One day something very special happened. The morning passed by just like every other morning. Many walked by, and a few dropped money in the plate. At noon, Patrick's mother stopped by to bring some lunch and check on him. She left about thirty minutes later. But at 3 P.M., everything suddenly changed.

Two ministers, Rev. Peter Smith and Rev. John Jacobs, were on their way to an important prayer meeting. Suddenly, they noticed this crippled young man with his plaintive sign leaning against him. Rev. Smith motioned to his colleague to join him as they approached Patrick. Both men felt deep compassion for this young man.

"Good afternoon, son. Would you look at the two of us?" asked Peter Smith.

Instinctively, Patrick turned toward them with his plate held high. He was pretty confident that these two fine ministers would offer their financial assistance.

Seeing the pan, Peter smiled and then said, "Well, young man, we really don't have any cash to give you, but what we do have we will give freely to you."

Great, Patrick was thinking to himself. *Another lecture about religion, or my need to repent of my sins. Doesn't he know that my greatest need is financial?*

Then Rev. Smith issued this remarkable command: "In the name of Jesus Christ of Nazareth, get up and walk!"

Instantly, nerve tissue was repaired. Muscle was rebuilt at the blink of an eye. The ankles were made whole. Without having even one moment's practice, and without even a hint of a wobble, Patrick jumped to his feet and began to walk. In his exuberance, he began to jump up and down giving praise to God for the miracle that had taken place. John Jacobs and Peter Smith watched with pure delight.

The local NBC affiliate beat both CNN and Patrick's parents to the temple courts for the first interview. Satellite dishes, helicopters and reporters started arriving from every direction as the word spread about this irrefutable supernatural occurrence. Patrick had his arms on the shoulders of the two ministers as cameras and microphones were being set up. Several eyewitnesses pointed to the Rev. Peter Smith as the miracle worker, and the media crush zoomed in on him.

"What is your name, sir, and just what is going on here?" asked one reporter.

"My name is Rev. Peter Smith, and this is my colleague, Rev. John Jacobs. Just a few minutes ago, Jesus Christ healed this young man who has been crippled from birth."

The reporters looked at each other quizzically as they wondered who would ask the next obvious question.

"Wait a minute, Reverend. Are you telling us that this man was instantly healed by some kind of divine intervention, when our best doctors could be of no assistance? How can we be sure that he was ever really crippled? Couldn't this be just another religious hoax?"

A distinguished older gentleman pushed his way toward the cameras. Staring into the sea of lenses, he spoke: "My name is Dr. Philip Thompson. I have been the physician for Patrick and his family since the day he was born. In fact, I delivered him as a baby. I have the X-rays to prove his birth defect and its degenerative effect on him. I must say that I am as confounded as the rest of you. But don't waste your time trying to prove that this is some kind of hoax. His condition was hopeless until today."

As the cameras shifted back toward Patrick, Rev. Smith challenged the reporters and the large audience that had quickly gathered: "Why does this surprise you so much? Why do you feel this need to associate me or my colleague with this miracle? We could not possibly be responsible for this dramatic healing! The God of Abraham, Isaac and Jacob has simply glorified His servant Jesus. It is by faith in the strong name of Jesus Christ that this young man was restored to complete health."

Eventually, the crowds, reporters and cameras dissipated. All agreed that the second most phenomenal occurrence of the afternoon was this: given their "fifteen minutes of fame," neither Rev. Smith nor Rev. Jacobs took the opportunity to enhance their career, sell a book or accept offers for the movie rights. These ministers gave all the glory to Jesus Christ while removing themselves completely from the credit. This was almost as impressive as the healing itself.

This may not have happened in New York City, but this remarkable event actually did take place through the ministry of the apostles Peter and John in Acts 3:1-16. I have simply updated the material.

Try to enter into the emotion of this moment when the crippled beggar is instantly, permanently healed. What was it like to be able to walk, jump and run after years of sitting and watching others move freely about? How did it feel to be able to transport himself and no longer depend on others to carry him? It must have been a passionate experience of complete and utter joy: "Then he went with them into the temple courts, walking and jumping, and praising God" (Acts 3:8).

Just as overwhelming joy was the natural reaction of the crippled beggar in Acts 3, we can expect joy as we enter the family of God through faith in Christ. Salvation is very much like being healed. We had been crippled by the effects of sin. We were helpless and hopeless in our attempt to save ourselves, just as this man could not obtain strength in his ankles through self-effort. He needed and we needed a power from the outside to come inside and transform us. When that happens, we become the recipients of God's gift of salvation and partakers of what Peter calls "inexpressible and glorious joy" (1 Peter 1:8).

JOY IN OUR FORGIVENESS

What was discussed in chapter 1 is truly a cause for joy and celebration! Though unexpected, unearned and certainly undeserved, we have been forgiven. This is better than winning a million dollars! This is greater than any physical healing you could experience. It outranks any important news that we have ever received. The Almighty God of the universe has declared that our sins have been atoned for, our guilt is absolved and we have been completely forgiven.

And this is all in keeping with the biblical pattern. Joy comes through our mourning. When we deal with sin in our lives, that brokenness produces a genuine soul satisfaction. David realized this truth in Psalm 51:

> Hide your face from my sins
> and blot out all my iniquity.
> Create in me a pure heart, O God,
> and renew a steadfast spirit within me.
> Do not cast me from your presence
> or take your Holy Spirit from me.
> Restore to me the joy of your salvation
> and grant me a willing spirit, to sustain
> me. (Psalm 51:9-12)

As we confess and forsake iniquity, joy flows into the human heart. Jesus expressed it this way in His famous Sermon on the Mount, "Blessed are those who mourn, for they will be comforted" (Matthew 5:4). Or as the psalmist puts it, "Those who sow in tears will reap with songs of joy" (Psalm 126:5).

JOY IN OUR NEW STANDING WITH GOD

Because Christ has forgiven us, we now have a totally new standing with the Father. We now have direct access to God because of our advocate, His Son: "If anybody does sin, we have one who speaks to the Father in our defense—Jesus Christ, the Righteous One. He is the atoning sacrifice for our sins" (1 John 2:1-2).

Max Lucado illustrates this thrilling truth:

Christ meets you outside the throne room, takes you by the hand, and walks you into the presence of God. Upon entrance, we find grace, not condemnation; mercy, not punishment. Where we would never be granted an audience with the King, we are now welcomed into His presence.

If you are a parent you understand this. If a child you don't know appears on your doorstep and asks to spend the night, what would you do? Likely, you would ask him his name, where he lives, find out why he is roaming the streets, and contact his parents. On the other hand, if a youngster enters your house escorted by your child, that child is welcome. The same is true with

God. By becoming friends with the Son we gain access to the Father.[1]

Our new standing is that of a son or daughter in the family of God. Christ paid for and signed the adoption papers with His own blood. Just like a child in an orphanage is filled with gratitude and joy when he becomes a member of his new family, we, too, can rejoice in our new position.

JOY FOR THE LONG HAUL

Jesus described the context of the long-term joy we can expect as members of His family:

> As the Father has loved me, so have I loved you. Now remain in my love, If you obey my commands, you will remain in my love, just as I have obeyed my Father's commands and remain in his love. I have told you this so that my joy may be in you and that your joy may be complete. (John 15:9-11)

"I have told you this" is a reference to what directly precedes, namely the concepts of "remaining" and "obeying." Our continuation in the "joy of the Lord" will be dependent, in part, on our commitment to "remain" in His love and "obey" His commands. This is similar to Paul's reminder that the Lord will "guard what I have entrusted to him for that day" (2 Timothy 1:12).

As we keep on entrusting our lives to Jesus, He will keep on guarding us.

This is powerfully illustrated in the life of our Lord. It was because of His obedience to the will of His Father in dying on the cross that the writer of Hebrews could say, "Let us fix our eyes on Jesus, the author and perfecter of our faith, who for the joy set before him endured the cross, scorning its shame, and sat down at the right hand of the throne of God" (Hebrews 12:2).

"Joy" and "enduring the cross" would appear to be an oxymoron. But the Savior delighted to do His Father's will. There was joy in His deference to God's plan for salvation.

Many Christians who lose their experience of joy in their Christian walk have failed to fulfill their responsibility. They wander off into sin in clear disobedience to the will of God and then wonder why they don't sense the deep and abiding joy promised by the Savior. But this spiritual bliss is reserved for those who remain and obey.

Other believers become disillusioned about their lack of joy because they have confused joy with "happiness." They had hoped that the Christian life would be one "happy" day after another. But happiness, in this sense of the word, is a purely emotional response to outward circumstances—or, as someone has said, "Happiness depends on happenings." If the events of a person's life are going his or her way, that person can be happy; otherwise, sadness sets in. This leads to a roller-coaster experience of highs and lows, which can become quite exhausting.

Joy, on the other hand, is not primarily *emotional*. More than mere *feeling*, joy is a *fact* based on the truth about God, His love for us and His acceptance of us. Facts are stubborn things. They don't fluctuate back and forth or up and down. Outwardly, things may be falling apart, but inwardly, we can bask in His love. Joy has to do with deep, internal realities; happiness focuses on surface external emotions. This is why, even under excruciating circumstances, we can still maintain joy in our hearts.

Of course, there is difference between joy *in the midst of* a difficulty and joy *because of* a tough situation. God does not, for example, expect us to rejoice *because of* an auto accident—that would be total nonsense! But we can rejoice *in the midst of* that accident because of what God may teach us through the experience.

An illustration of this can be found in Acts 13. False rumors were spreading among the leaders in Antioch, and this led to the persecution and expulsion of Paul and Barnabas. Look how the believers reacted to these troubling times: "So they shook the dust from their feet in protest against them and went to Iconium. And the disciples were filled with joy and with the Holy Spirit" (Acts 13:51-52).

This is rejoicing *in* tribulation, not *for* it. They were not smiling about the fact that Paul and Barnabas were persecuted and expelled. But they were able to be filled with joy because of what God would do as a result of their troubles.

The closing phrase of John 15:11 is "that your joy may be complete." One implication of this is that a false, short-term, incomplete joy does indeed exist in the world. There is a counterfeit version which lacks longevity and wholeness. The Bible reminds us that it is possible "to enjoy the pleasures of sin for a short time" (Hebrews 11:25). Solomon's lament in this regard is rather compelling:

> I denied myself nothing my eyes desired;
> I refused my heart no pleasure. . . .
> Yet when I surveyed all that my hands had
> done
> and what I had toiled to achieve,
> everything was meaningless, a chasing after
> the wind;
> nothing was gained under the sun.
> (Ecclesiastes 2:10-11)

In contrast to this, David announces, "You have made known to me the path of life; you will fill me with joy in your presence, with eternal pleasures at your right hand" (Psalm 16:11).

This is what to expect as a Christian: joy for the long haul. This deep sense of delight can be our experience in "the sweet by-and-by," but also in "the nasty here and now." Christ has provided for it, and we can revel in it.

JOY IN OUR DEMEANOR

"Are you happy in the Lord?" she asked.

"Of course I am!" he said.

"Well then, perhaps you should tell your face about it," she replied.

This old joke serves as a fresh reminder of this simple truth: the joy of the Lord should be evident in our lives. One reason that Jesus was accused of being "a glutton and a drunkard" (Matthew 11:19) was the unrelenting joy in His demeanor. Children were no doubt attracted to Him for this same reason. He was a frequent guest at banquets and parties. Though our Lord was also "a man of sorrows and acquainted with grief " because of His suffering for our sins, His public life was characterized by jubilation.

Let me clarify this by saying that we will not all express the joy of the Lord in the same manner. The differences in our personalities should prevent us from ever establishing a "standard for joyful demeanor." This is not a contest for the biggest smile or the loudest laugh. (In fact, a boisterous laugh can be an attempt to hide pain and sorrow.)

But regardless of our personality or style, people should be able to sense this joy in our daily lives.

I have met many Christians in my travels who do not in any way reflect the joy of the Lord. Some of them are respected Christian leaders. Their faces are frozen in a frown, and they most often speak in a negative, abrasive manner. Perhaps they even believe that it is a mark of true holiness to have a sour, angry disposition. But this does not make for an attractive ambassador for the One who said, "I have told you this so that my joy may be in you and that your joy may be complete" (John 15:11).

Not only can we expect the joy of the Lord to be in our hearts as Christians, we can also expect that it will be demonstrated through our jubilant demeanor. At times, it may be "joy unspeakable," but it should never be "joy unnoticeable." Indeed, we should tell our face about the joy in our hearts.

THE JOY EPIDEMIC

I once saw a poster which said, "Joy is contagious—let's start an epidemic!"

My father's life illustrated this. Contagious joy was an aura about him. He just had a way of brightening the mood wherever he went. It took real effort not to smile when he made his entrance. He deeply loved God, he energetically loved life, and he genuinely loved people. And those who knew him could "feel" this reality. Bill Allen delighted in his ability to spread the joy of the Lord to others.

My father was no stranger to somber moods and down days. But the general tone of his life was that intimate, complete, enduring joy that comes from being rightly related to God. He would often quote the words of the famous Nazarene preacher, "Uncle Bud" Robinson: "I'm as happy as a bald-headed bumble bee in forty acres of clover!"

His joyful demeanor spread like a good disease to lonely, elderly people in nursing homes. It touched those who were wounded in difficult marriages. The contagion impacted those who were saddened by the consequences of sin—it called them to the joy of repentance and the freedom of forgiveness.

Perhaps you have been privileged to experience the contagious joy of the Lord through someone you have known. There was just that special sense of delight in his or her presence. You enjoyed being with that person because of the way in which you were lifted out of your own despair.

We must go beyond merely being thankful for having known someone like this. By God's grace, we should get infected with that same blessed disease—and become a carrier! Joy-filled lives can be used by God to touch a sad world caught in the clutches of despair.

What can you expect now that you've become a Christian? Expect joy! Joy that is genuine and longlasting. Joy that is deeper than any happiness you've ever experienced. Joy that can so infiltrate your own heart that it spills over to bless others. Expect to catch the joy bug—and then go out and start an epidemic!

ENDNOTE

[1] Max Lucado, *In the Grip of Grace* (Dallas, TX: Word, 1996), p. 93.

CHAPTER 3

Expect
Peace

They were in a boat off the Florida coast. Thirteen were on board that day. Many of them were experienced sailors, and they knew this part of the ocean like the back of their hands. The weather appeared to be good for the journey.

Suddenly, to their complete surprise, a furious squall seemed to come out of nowhere, bringing with it ten- to fifteen-foot waves, fierce winds and widespread lightning. Using every possible maneuver they had ever learned, they coped with the storm as best they could. But the possibility of safely reaching shore seemed remote.

Then they realized that one of the passengers was missing. Where was that preacher, anyway? Couldn't he offer a prayer for safety or something, before the boat breaks apart and everyone falls in the sea?

They finally found him in the stern of the boat—sound asleep! The sailors looked at each other in utter dismay. How could he possibly sleep through this?

One of the crew angrily shook him while shouting, "Don't you care if we all drown? How dare you sleep during this crisis! Get up right now and help! Pray! Do something!"

The preacher sat up, rubbed his eyes and shook his head. Then he casually strolled to the upper deck and looked out over the storm. He spoke directly to the wind and the waves with these words: "Peace—be still!" Instantaneously, every molecule of water became as flat as glass. The wind speed dropped from 60 mph to 0 mph in the blink of an eye. The ocean was utterly calm under a perfectly blue sky. "Who is this guy?" the sailors asked each other. "Even the wind and the waves obey him!"

No, this didn't really happen off the Florida coast; it was on the Sea of Galilee. This story from Mark 4:35-41 underlines the fact that we can expect peace when we join the family of God. We can experience this holy tranquillity even in the midst of life's troubles—as Jesus so eloquently illustrates by snoring through the storm. Even when everyone around us is fretting and faithless like the doubting disciples, we can know "the peace of God, which transcends all understanding" (Philippians 4:7).

PEACE BECAUSE OF . . .

Why should we "expect peace" in our hearts and lives when we become Christians? The apostle Paul lays out the answer for us:

> For he himself is our peace, who has made the two one and has destroyed the barrier, the dividing wall of hostility, by abolishing in his flesh the law with its commandments and regulations. His purpose was to create in himself one new man out of the two, thus making peace, and in this one body to reconcile both of them to God through the cross, by which he put to death their hostility. He came and preached peace to you who were far away and peace to those who were near. For through him we both have access to the Father by one Spirit. (Ephesians 2:14-18)

In the context, the "two" is a reference to Jews and Gentiles. Christ's death and resurrection have once and for all destroyed the dividing wall between these two factions because salvation would no longer be provided on the basis of one's heritage. Jesus has made it possible for all people, regardless of their religious background, to become a part of His family and know peace with God through simple faith in His shed blood.

We can expect peace in our hearts because of the cross work of Christ. Though our sins set a holy God against us, the Savior paid the price for those sins and gave us a clean slate. Just as a clean, white glove can cover a dirty hand, Jehovah only sees the purity of His Son when He looks at us. Now we are declared righteous in the presence of God because Jesus said so. The war is over. Peace is ours to enjoy here and hereafter.

Let us never forget that the peace we delight in came at a great cost. Jesus Christ had to go to war on our behalf. He had to endure His Father's rejection so that we could enjoy His Father's acceptance. Our Lord went through excruciating sorrow and suffering so that we could experience joy and peace. We can expect peace because of the Savior's willingness to take God's wrath in our place.

PEACE INSTEAD OF . . .

We can also expect real peace instead of the counterfeit version. "Peace I leave with you; my peace I give you," Jesus said. "I do not give to you as the world gives. Do not let your hearts be troubled and do not be afraid" (John 14:27).

Christ clearly tells us here that the world offers a rendition of peace that is not to be confused with what He calls "my peace." Maybe you can remember a certain kind of tranquillity that you enjoyed before you were a Christian. Perhaps it was based on material success, career satisfaction, marital contentment or some other positive external circumstance. But this is not the kind of peace that reaches deep into the heart.

Without peace with God, it really doesn't matter how many material possessions we may have. We may have the best job in the world, a wonderful spouse and children and many other perks and privileges. But if we have not settled the sin issue, it will always be in the back of our minds, robbing us of genuine *soul* peace. Paul gives us the reason for this spiritual paranoia:

> The wrath of God is being revealed from heaven against all the godlessness and wickedness of men who suppress the truth by their wickedness, since what may be known about God is plain to them, because God has made it plain to them. For since the creation of the world God's invisible qualities—his eternal power and divine nature—have been clearly seen, being understood from what has been made, so that men are without excuse. (Romans 1:18-20)

The apostle declares that we are "without excuse" for ignoring God and His righteous demands on our lives. His presence and power are more than obvious to anyone who will take the time to study His creation.

Paul also says that God's wrath "is being revealed" in the lives of those who reject the Lord. In one sense that is taking place right now in the form of discontentment—the lack of real peace. Those outside of Christ realize that something is not quite right even though they seem to have everything that should give them serenity. What they really long for is this elusive peace of the soul.

The root of this discontent is seen in Solomon's lament that God "has set eternity in the hearts of men" (Ecclesiastes 3:11). The eternal quality of the human soul—of something beyond the grave—is equally inescapable for those who believe in God and those who do not. We have a built-in urgency to be "at peace" with regard to the afterlife.

Only salvation through the blood of Jesus Christ can give us peace with God in this world, and the peace of God for the world to come. It's part of the package we receive as members of God's family. It's why there is such an incredible contrast between the dying moments of the believer and the unbeliever: one is calm and confident, the other edgy and uncertain.

My mother died after a five-year battle with Hepatitis C. On the Thursday before her death, she told us with peace and confidence that she was going to be with Jesus and her husband on Sunday. She did just that on Mother's Day of 1994. Mom had peace with God as well as the peace of God. She had this instead of the peace the world offers.

PEACE IN SPITE OF . . .

In Acts 27:13-44, we see another story of terror at sea. It is a picture of unrelenting chaos and turmoil as the crew wrestles hopelessly against a hurricane. Food and water have been thrown overboard in an effort to lighten the ship. Just when the mood has reached its lowest point, Paul pipes up with this cheery announcement: "I told you so! You could have saved yourselves from all this damage and loss if you had just listened to me back there in Crete."

Can you imagine the reaction of this crew? This was a dangerous group of men because the text tells us that they "had gone a long time without food." Talk about a tough audience! Paul was either very brave or very stupid to make a statement like that!

As it turns out, he was brave. Twice he told the sailors to "keep up your courage," and personally guaranteed the safety of everyone on board. Because of the message he received from an angel, Paul was at peace, in spite of the dire circumstances surrounding him. The end result? "Everyone reached land in safety."

We, too, can know this "in spite of" peace from God. Listen to Paul's description of this lifestyle:

> . . . I have learned to be content whatever the circumstances. I know what it is to be in need, and I know what it is to have plenty. I have learned the secret of being content in any and every situation, whether well fed or hungry, whether living in plenty or in want. I can do everything through him who gives me strength. (Philippians 4:11-13)

As was pointed out in the last chapter, the apostle's contentment in any and every situation did not necessarily mean that he "liked" or "enjoyed" or "felt at peace" about each predicament of his life! He had learned, however, to maintain the peace of God deep in his heart regardless of circumstances. In Christ, he could put up with anything and everything that came his way.

We may not "feel at peace" with every twist and turn of the road in our Christian walk, and there is no reason to pretend otherwise. We should never feel obligated to say things like, "I have peace about the tragic car accident that killed my friend." Nevertheless, God can give us His peace, "which transcends all understanding" (4:7), even in the midst of our pain.

PEACEMAKERS

We can enjoy peace because of, instead of and in spite of. A natural response to this would be the passion to become a peacemaker. Those who get peace should want to give it to others. Jesus tells us, "Blessed are the peacemakers, for they will be called sons of God" (Matthew 5:9). One proof that we have been born again is this wonderful peace of God in our lives and the longing for others to know the same deep soul serenity. We want to facilitate the peace process whenever and wherever possible.

It should be noted, however, that there is a difference between a peace*maker* and a peace*keeper*. A peacekeeper will do anything to "keep the peace"—including lying, deception, misrepresentation, whitewashing or covering up—anything to keep a lid on a problem. Rather than face a given situation with the truth and its nasty ramifications, the peacekeeper tries to smooth things over.

The peacemaker, on the other hand, is committed to genuine, enduring peace. This person confronts conflict in a straightforward manner so that when a settlement is reached, it is the real deal. Without being unwise or reckless, the peacemaker is willing to take an unpopular stand on his or her way to achieving an authentic peace.

Our Lord alluded to this distinction when He said,

Do not suppose that I have come to bring peace to the earth. I did not come to bring peace, but a sword. For I have come to turn

> " 'a man against his father,
> a daughter against her mother,
> a daughter-in-law against her
> mother-in-law—
> a man's enemies will be the members of
> his own household.' " (10:34-36)

This is what happens when some members of a family embrace Christ as their Savior but others do not. In this instance the Savior is not an instrument of peace, but a sword which divides a family. This leads to incredible conflict between spouses and children. Any attempt to "keep the peace" in this scenario will not last because the battle lines have been drawn in the spiritual realm.

Paul made this same point in Romans 12:18: "If it is possible, as far as it depends on you, live at peace with everyone." The implication is clear. It will not always be possible to "live at peace with everyone." Some people will choose to hate and abuse us. They do not want to be reconciled with us even when we reach out to them in love. The apostle tells us to let it go. We must accept the fact that not everyone wants a peaceful relationship.

MAINTAINING THE PEACE

The prophet Isaiah gives us the secret to maintaining the peace of God in our Christian walk: "You will keep in perfect peace him whose mind is steadfast, because he trusts in you" (Isaiah 26:3). As we focus our minds on the Lord Himself and put our trust completely in Him, we will preserve this blessed tranquility in our hearts. When we let our minds wander to our circumstances and allow our faith to be placed in sources other than God Himself, we will lose our peace.

Think of a little boy walking through a dark cave with his father. As long as he keeps focused on Dad and walks closely behind, he will have nothing to fear. But if that boy allows himself to look back, he will suddenly lose that sense of security in the darkness behind him. And if he strays down another path in that cavern and gets out of his father's presence, he will really know what it means to be afraid.

It is the same in the spiritual realm. To sustain the peace of God, we must stay close to Him and keep our focus on Him alone.

PEACE AS THE UMPIRE

It's the bottom of the ninth; the score is 2-2, with a runner on second. Three balls, two strikes. The pitcher winds up and lets it go. A loud "crack" is heard. It's a looping base hit into shallow right field. The outfield defense has a reputation for throwing runners out at home plate. The third base coach is processing all of this as the runner from second approaches third, waiting for his signal. The arm begins waving wildly in a circular motion sending the base runner home for what may be the winning score.

Those last ninety feet seem like 10,000 as he rounds third. The ball is well on its way to the catcher, who waits eagerly for the sound of leather on leather and braces for the inevitable collision. Dust begins to billow as the base runner hits the ground headfirst on a wild slide toward the plate. The ball has arrived from shallow right. Commotion prevails at home plate under a brown and white cloud of dust and line chalk. The umpire waits for one brief, dramatic moment before rendering his verdict. "Safe!" he screams, his arms shifting back and forth in a horizontal slice. The umpire has spoken. There is no court of appeals. The game is over, the score 3-2.

There is a verse in Scripture that correlates with the dramatic conclusion to this baseball game: "Let the peace of Christ rule in your hearts" (Colossians 3:15). The Greek word for "rule" is literally "umpire" or "referee." Paul is saying, "Let the peace of our Lord Jesus be the umpire in your hearts." The calm of Christ is to be the final arbiter. When we have determined that we have His peace about a decision, we can move ahead with confidence. We do not need to worry about the outcome. His peace has had the final say.

It is possible to arrive at a sense of "peace" through human manipulation or self-deception. We can talk ourselves into just about anything in the name of the Lord. That's why our decisions must also pass the tests of Scripture, the wisdom of many counselors and good, Spirit-anointed common sense. It's not enough to simply say, "I have peace about it."

I have known pastors who claimed to have "peace" about a call to a new or different role in ministry. Not surprisingly, it is often a larger position with more financial security. But clear instruction from God's Word, combined with solid, unemotional reasoning and the advice of associates would and should overrule this pseudoserenity. Only when this peace of God lines up with Scripture, trusted advisors and sound judgment can we rest in the assurance that we are moving in God's will. Peace at last.

Without this peace of God, we should not move ahead with any plan or decision. We should wait on the Lord patiently until we have the unruffled assurance that we are going with the flow of His Spirit. And when that deep soul serenity arrives, we can forge ahead and trust God for great things.

Does the peace of God rule in your heart? Are you listening carefully for His approval and blessing, or have you settled for the voice of human persuasion and coercion? Our Lord is gracious. He will let us know when we are missing the mark by giving us that "divine discomfort." And we should proceed with caution until His peace returns.

Now that you believe, expect peace. Expect it because of what Christ has provided. Expect His peace instead of the false, tenuous version which circulates in our world. Expect it in spite of unsettling circumstances. As the umpire in your soul, God's peace shouts, "SAFE!"

CHAPTER 4

Expect Trials

*H*er name was Rhoda. Her husband's name was Jim. They had two young children when they discovered that she had a very serious form of cancer. In a matter of months, this wife and mother, still in her twenties, was dead.

Jim was an elder in the church and a respected man of God. Rhoda was a godly woman whom everyone seemed to like. Life was going along just fine; she had a family that loved her, a nice home and many friends to enjoy. But suddenly, strange symptoms surfaced; the diagnosis of cancer was announced. Only a few months were available to say good-bye. The funeral took place. Somehow, life goes on for the survivors.

I was just a teenager when this happened to a family in my father's church. It was shocking at the time, and it still seems like a strange occurrence to me. But since then, I have discovered that this same painful scenario is played out every day in homes throughout the country.

How could this happen to a wonderful Christian couple who were committed fully to the Lord? Was God mad at Jim or Rhoda—or both of them? Why this young mother and not someone else? Was a "secret sin" the cause of her cancer? If this could happen to a nice person like Rhoda, are any of us safe?

Troubling questions. They become even more puzzling for the person who is in the midst of the trial.

GOOD NEWS AND BAD NEWS

The first three chapters of this book represent the "good news"—that we can expect forgiveness, joy and peace now that we are Christians. Chapters 4–7 deal with what may appear to be the "bad news"—that we can also expect trials, temptation, persecution and doubts. We will learn that this is not really bad news, because God has something good in store for us even during difficult times.

Several Scriptures indicate that trials in your life and mine are a matter of when, not if: "Consider it pure joy, my brothers, whenever you face trials . . ." (James 1:2); "In this world you will have trouble" (John 16:33); "We must go through many hardships to enter the kingdom of God" (Acts 14:22).

Even though we know that we should "expect" difficulty from time to time, we usually react in ways that indicate it was totally unexpected. The inevitability of trials never quite sinks in. We always seem to be reaching for that stress-free, hassle-free, tribulation-free life that doesn't really exist on this earth. Though we may enjoy periods of relative calm, no one can claim a permanent exemption from affliction.

We can also expect the trials in our lives to seem unfair at times. In the game of football, it is against the rules to "pile on" the man with the ball once he has been tackled and the whistle has blown. No such rule exists for trials! Some people appear to have a greater number of hardships, at a deeper level of intensity; the trials just seem to "pile on top" of one another. Why? This is a mystery that won't be solved until we reach the other shore.

Most of the time there is no explanation for this unbalanced occurrence. It could hardly be considered "fair" by any stretch. Some folks seem to sail through life with only brief, minor skirmishes along the way. Others face one ordeal after another in a seemingly unending procession of trouble.

BLAME IT ON ADAM AND EVE

Why do we live in a world where we must expect a certain amount of difficulty? One answer goes back to the very beginning:

To the woman he said,

"I will greatly increase your pains in
        childbearing;
    with pain you will give birth to children.
Your desire will be for your husband,
    and he will rule over you."

To Adam he said, "Because you listened to
your wife and ate from the tree about which I
commanded you, 'You must not eat of it,'

"Cursed is the ground because of you;
    through painful toil you will eat of it all the
    days of your life.
It will produce thorns and thistles for you,
    and you will eat the plants of the field.
By the sweat of your brow
    you will eat your food
until you return to the ground,
    since from it you were taken;
for dust you are
    and to dust you will return."

(Genesis 3:16-19)

The thorns and weeds in our gardens, along
with the thorns and weeds in our daily lives, can be
traced back to this critical moment in human his-
tory. The fall of Adam and Eve permanently
changed the course of our existence. Shortly after

this pronouncement of doom, Cain, the first child born, murdered his little brother Abel. Things got off to a bad start, and it's been downhill ever since. Trials exist because of original sin.

At times, the connection is vague and indirect. The young mother in my introduction who died from the ravages of cancer was not being punished for committing a particular sin. But there is a sense in which cancer and all of the other illnesses in our world today are the outcome of Adam and Eve's insistence on disobedience in the Garden of Eden. This was a devastatingly defining moment. Sin, coupled with Satan's limited power, were unleashed that day at the very beginning of creation.

Sometimes there *is* a direct link between iniquity and affliction, although the ramifications may reach beyond the guilty party. A man gets drunk, gets behind the wheel of a car and kills someone. His sins of overindulgence and breaking the law result in a series of trials for himself—but also for the family of his innocent victim. They will struggle with that tragedy as long as they live.

This is why the Bible is not quick to blame God for the fact that we can expect trials. Though He allows trying times and uses them in our lives, we should not assume that He is directly responsible for the trouble that comes our way. We are collectively accountable for our distraught world—from Adam and Eve to this present generation. Our disobedience

has created an atmosphere in which adversity must
be anticipated.

GOD MAY BRING TRIALS

But some trials exist because God orchestrates
them.

Is it right to say, "God gave me this hardship"? At
times, the answer is yes. The suffering of Job is referred to as "all the trouble the LORD had brought
upon him" (Job 42:11). The Lord can and will use
disease or disaster to draw us closer to Himself. He
may even cause these things to happen for His
greater purpose in our lives.

Listen to Paul's explanation of his own life of
hardship:

> To keep me from becoming conceited be-
> cause of these surpassingly great revelations,
> there was given me a thorn in my flesh, a mes-
> senger of Satan, to torment me. Three times I
> pleaded with the Lord to take it away from
> me. But he said to me, "My grace is sufficient
> for you, for my power is made perfect in
> weakness." Therefore I will boast all the more
> gladly about my weaknesses, so that Christ's
> power may rest on me. That is why, for
> Christ's sake, I delight in weaknesses, in in-
> sults, in hardships, in persecutions, in difficul-

ties. For when I am weak, then I am strong. (2 Corinthians 12:7-10)

I saw this Scripture in the life of a man by the name of Chuck Russell. He was a rebellious guy from his earliest days. Chuck would get deep into a life of crime, get caught by the police, serve some time in jail and come back to the Lord. This cycle was repeated several times. Then one day, everything changed.

Shortly after Chuck's fortieth birthday, he was diagnosed with multiple sclerosis. I visited him during the last week of his life and I'll never forget something he whispered in my ear: "Tom, God gave me M.S. out of His great mercy. He didn't want me to backslide anymore. I'm ready to go and be with the Lord." Though this is an extreme case, it illustrates the "severe mercy" of our God as He disciplines His children.

Many people become bitter at God because of the tough times they are facing, but their anger is misplaced. Even if the Lord is directly responsible, as in the preceding story, it is ultimately for their own benefit. Joseph could say this to the brothers who sold him into slavery, "You intended to harm me, but God intended it for good to accomplish what is now being done, the saving of many lives" (Genesis 50:20).

In Job 1:1-12, we see how the Lord God allowed His servant Job to be tested by Satan. This man went through unbelievable trials and tribulations including the death of family members, the loss of his health and the destruction of his property. He was tempted to blame God for randomly selecting him to suffer. But in the end, he found great comfort and consolation in the wisdom and plan of God. "I know that you can do all things; no plan of yours can be thwarted. . . . My ears had heard of you but now my eyes have seen you" (Job 42:2,5).

Job could see at the end what he could never envision at the beginning.

WE MAY BRING TRIALS ON OURSELVES

Trials also exist because of human error.

It is all too possible to create our own hardships through unwise decisions. For example, some people experience financial problems because of extravagant spending. God did not bring this "trial of debt" upon them. It's not the result of Adam and Eve's fall from grace. It was the natural consequence of poor money management.

If I seek a job or ministry for which I am unqualified, with enough political savvy I might even obtain that new position. But the turmoil that follows this kind of folly will be of my own making. I dare not call it a "trial from the Lord" or even a "trial from the devil" when I come crashing down. It's the logical outcome for someone who maneuvers himself into places where he doesn't belong.

Isn't this why eternity in heaven sounds so good to us? It will be just the opposite of our painful experience here. Our lives really do last just a "few days" and they are "full of trouble" (Job 14:1). But someday we will be able to expect perfection—freedom from every nasty disappointment. No more tears, no more trials, no more imperfection! What a glorious hope!

THE PURPOSE OF TRIALS

Can you find the common thread that weaves its way through these passages of Scripture?

> Consider it pure joy, my brothers, whenever you face trials of many kinds, because you know that the testing of your faith develops perseverance. Perseverance must finish its work so that you may be mature and complete, not lacking anything. (James 1:2-4)

> In this you greatly rejoice, though now for a little while you may have had to suffer grief in all kinds of trials. These have come so that your faith—of greater worth than gold, which perishes even though refined by fire—may be proved genuine and may re-

sult in praise, glory and honor when Jesus Christ is revealed. (1 Peter 1:6-7)

And we know that in all things God works for the good of those who love him, who have been called according to his purpose. For those God foreknew he also predestined to be conformed to the likeness of his Son, that he might be the firstborn among many brothers. (Romans 8:28-29)

The key phrases that tie these passages together are "mature and complete" (James), "proved genuine" (1 Peter), and "conformed to the likeness of his Son" (Romans). The purpose of trials is to goad us toward godliness. The Lord uses hardship in our lives to move us in the direction of maturity—in essence, to make us more like Jesus Christ.

Christians often quote Romans 8:28 way out of context. They see someone going through difficulty and then say with a faint smile, "You know, all things work together for our good." That doesn't mean much to the individual who is suffering! They need to know what the word "good" refers to in the context. And we find out exactly what's "good" about trials in the next verse. God's plan is to use the circumstances of our lives, both positive and negative, to shape us into the image of His dear Son.

Though it may not entirely remove the sting of the painful things we go through, it is wonderful to know that the Lord can orchestrate each and every trial so that we become more like Jesus. Knowing this helps us accept the apparent randomness of the bad things that happen to good people. Everything can work in a positive direction. Even the foolish mistakes that we bring upon ourselves can be redeemed in this process of developing Christlikeness.

We usually say things like this when facing tough times: "Lord, why did this happen to me?" Perhaps a more appropriate question is, "Lord, in what way are You going to use this in my life to make me more like You?" In His time the Savior will answer this inquiry. We will begin to see measurable maturity, a more genuine faith and a lifestyle that more resembles our Lord.

Can you see the hand of God in some difficulty you have faced or may now be facing? Though it is rare to see the "good" thing the Lord is doing while we are in the midst of the mayhem, it will eventually be revealed—if not in this world, in the world to come. Patience is a virtue.

RESPONDING TO TRIALS

We have established the fact that hardship is to be expected in the Christian life. We have seen the origins of our trials and their intended purpose. But it is possible to know these things intellectually without accepting them in our hearts. This most often leads to a sense of anger and betrayal when we are suffering in the midst of a trial. We are tempted to ask, "How could a loving God allow this to happen to me?"

Someone has wisely said that hardship will either make us bitter or better. If we refuse to acknowledge the hand of God in our negative circumstances, we can become cynical and old before our time. If we begin to believe that troubling times are meaningless, random events that happen to anyone at any time, we will become bitter toward God and others.

The Bible warns us, "See to it that . . . no bitter root grows up to cause trouble and defile many" (Hebrews 12:15). This is an interesting word picture. The root can look harmless enough at first. But given time, fertile soil and some water, it will expand until it becomes a real menace. Nursing grudges against others (including God) and being unwilling to admit our own wrongdoing is ideal "soil" and "water" for this root of bitterness. Eventually the acrimony grows until it becomes unmanageable—like a vine that takes over a forest.

The only "herbicide" for the root of bitterness is forgiveness and acceptance. The person going through the trial must be willing to forgive whoever inflicted the trial, even if this means forgiving oneself—or God! And then there must be an acceptance of the fact that, yes, God can even use hardship to bless us and make us better Christians.

Forgiving and accepting are easier for me to write about and for you to read about than they are for either of us to put into practice. Bitterness can appear to be a sweet morsel to be savored. Sometimes we think we might feel better if we just hang on to our ill feelings about a past or present trial. Over the long haul, however, it is always better to deal with that root of bitterness.

As I write this book, I am entering my twenty-fifth year of ministry. I have been knocked around quite a bit during the past two-and-a-half decades. I have certainly created enough of my own trials. Some hardships came from the Lord and others were inflicted upon me. I have "resigned" from my calling, on average, about once a month! But through it all, I've always made this simple request: "Lord, don't allow me to become bitter. Help me to deal with the real issues before that root can become firmly planted." By His grace, I have been able to keep a smile on my face.

How are you responding to the difficulties in your Christian walk? Have your trials made you bitter or better? Now might be just the right time to put this book down and offer a simple prayer to the Lord—something like this:

Lord, I acknowledge that I have allowed bitterness to become rooted in my heart because of the tough times I am facing. I want You to know that

I forgive those who may have brought about this trial and I choose to accept the fact that You will use these dire circumstances to make me more like You. I want to thank You for all the ways You intend to bring me to maturity.

We can expect trials because we live in a fallen world. We can rest assured that some of our difficulties will emanate from God Himself. And, most certainly, we will bring hardship upon ourselves because we are not perfect. But here's something else we can expect: Our Lord will be with us and for us in the midst of our adversity. He worded His bountiful promise this way: "Never will I leave you; never will I forsake you" (Hebrews 13:5).

There may be times we feel like the Savior has left us or forsaken us. This sensation of isolation from the love of God may seem very real to us. But it's a mirage of our emotions. God has declared his faithfulness to accompany us in both the good times and the bad. This is a cold, hard fact that cannot be budged. We may need to remind ourselves of this reality at those times when the "feeling" of His presence is missing.

Expect trials? Oh, yes. Expect God to be with us? Oh, YES!

CHAPTER 5

Expect Temptation

It was perhaps the most dramatic arrest of the decade in the Detroit metropolitan area. Police officers casually drove into a church parking lot and strolled up to the main entrance. Ten minutes later, they left through that same door with their suspect—the senior pastor—in handcuffs. He was charged with several counts of robbery.

The minister had robbed several banks in the area using a clever series of disguises. No one was ever hurt during these holdups. No guns were fired. He usually took just a few thousand dollars at each stop. Tellers said that he was unusually "nice" for a thief.

Why would a minister do such a thing? Was he not being paid well enough by his church? Did he have exorbitant medical bills that forced him to steal? Had he gotten into gambling and run up a huge debt? None of the above.

He robbed banks to pay for his sexual addiction. After years of struggling with pornography and massage parlors, this preacher succumbed to the next level of temptation—$1,000-a-night hookers. While pastoring a growing church and serving in a leadership role on the district executive committee for his denomination, this husband and father was burglarizing banks and having sex with prostitutes.

My brother Tim served on committees with this pastor and he called me the day that this story broke in the news. Tim was quite distraught over the fact that a coworker in the ministry could have gotten so deep into sin with no one even noticing until it was way too late. It was later discovered that he had actually robbed banks on the way to and from district functions.

It's a bizarre, extreme story in many ways. But when we understand the cyclical nature of temptation, yielding and subsequent addiction, we can more readily relate to what happened in the life of this pastor.

WE'RE ALL IN THE SAME BOAT

We can expect temptation. It is a part of life for every born-again believer. Warning His disciples, Jesus said, "Watch and pray so that you will not fall into temptation. The spirit is willing, but the body is weak" (Mark 14:38).

Jesus would not have commanded us to "watch and pray" if we were not susceptible to "falling into temptation." We are blessed with willing spirits, but our weak bodies do not always cooperate. This is not only true of those who have committed heinous crimes. It is true of you. It is true of me. "No temptation has seized you," Paul wrote, "except what is common to man" (1 Corinthians 10:13).

The devil would like us to believe that we are all alone in our battle with temptation, because we are more likely to give up when we feel lonely in the conflict. But as we examine our own experience and talk with other believers, we realize that we are truly in this struggle together. We may face different types of seduction, but the propensity for being seduced is within each of us.

The things that tantalize us may not lead to the depths of depravity described in the opening illustration. But the potential is there. For those who may doubt their capacity for evil, Jeremiah states it bluntly: "The heart is deceitful above all things and beyond cure. Who can understand it?" (Jeremiah 17:9).

A CRUCIAL DISTINCTION

In chapter 4, we looked at the issues of trials in the Christian life. But trials are not to be confused with temptation. Whereas God may impose hardship on His children to help them grow, He is never the source of temptation. James cleared this up once-and-for-all: "When tempted, no one should say, 'God is tempting me.' For God cannot be tempted by evil, nor does he tempt anyone" (James 1:13).

Our Lord distances Himself from this entire process, including: the initial temptation, the yielding and any subsequent addiction. It is impossible to lure God into any form of evil, and it is just as unthinkable to accuse Him of being the source of enticement. He cannot play even a minor role in the sin cycle because this would compromise God's utter holiness.

Some translations of the prayer our Lord taught His disciples are misleading. "Lead us not into temptation" (Matthew 6:13, KJV) appears to suggest that God sometimes *does* lead people "into temptation." But I think the New Living Translation captures the real meaning of Christ's words: "Don't let us yield to temptation." Though Jesus is not responsible for getting us into our fascination with sin, He can help us get out. We'll look at this aspect a little later in the chapter.

There is this crucial distinction, then, between trials and temptations. Though God can and will use both in our lives, He may sometimes be directly responsible for a trial in our lives. But our Lord is never to be blamed for our temptations or our yielding to them. God is absolute purity. He hates sin and could never be an accomplice for an evil cause.

If God is not the source of our temptations, *who or what is?* Consider three sources for the enticement to sin:

THE WORLD

First, temptation comes from the world. The fallen world in which we live is corrupt to its very core. A drive through any good-sized town demonstrates the great energy and expense that go into making money from various forms of temptation. Alcohol, tobacco, pornography, drugs, prostitution—you name it and you can have it in a matter of moments. The words of Jesus come to mind: "Woe to the world because of the things that cause people to sin! Such things must come, but woe to the man through whom they come!" (Matthew 18:7).

Christ points out that judgment will someday fall—and not just on those who have yielded to temptation. Those who produce and sell the enticements will also answer to God for their actions. "Woe to the man through whom they come!"

John gives this warning to believers:

> Do not love the world or anything in the world. If anyone loves the world, the love of the Father is not in him. For everything in the world—the cravings of sinful man, the lust of his eyes and the boasting of what he has and does—comes not from the Father

but from the world. The world and its desires pass away, but the man who does the
will of God lives forever. (1 John 2:15-17)

The world in which we live is actually a breeding
ground for the three most basic sins: pride, sexual
lust and materialism. Just about any evil we can
think of emanates from these core iniquities. And
this is what characterizes the world in which we live.
As Christians, we must not embrace this corrupt
value system because it can only lead to spiritual disaster. Peter discusses this issue in his second letter:

His divine power has given us everything we
need for life and godliness through our knowledge of him who called us by his own glory and
goodness. Through these he has given us his
very great and precious promises, so that
through them you may participate in the divine
nature and escape the corruption in the world
caused by evil desires. (2 Peter 1:3-4)

Inherent in our world, says the apostle Peter,
are "evil desires" which have corrupted the entire
system. Whether we like it or not makes no difference. This is a cold, hard fact of existence. Though
it began in the garden of Eden with the disobedience of two individuals, the depravity has only
been compounded by the passing of time. The

temptation to commit some kind of sin literally lurks around every corner.

There are times when each of us has contemplated some kind of "escape" from the world into a monastery or another secluded setting. But even the monks would tell us that this is not a permanent evasion of temptation. It's not just the world "out there" that causes sinful enticement. We carry some elements of this evil domain in our hearts. We may remove ourselves physically from the population, but we would find it difficult to run completely away from our worldly hearts.

THE DEVIL

Second, temptation comes from Satan. The temptation of Eve serves as our best example here:

> Now the serpent was more crafty than any of the wild animals the LORD God had made. He said to the woman, "Did God really say, 'You must not eat from any tree in the garden'?"
>
> The woman said to the serpent, "We may eat fruit from the trees in the garden, but God did say, 'You must not eat fruit from the tree that is in the middle of the garden, and you must not touch it, or you will die.' "
>
> "You will not surely die," the serpent said to the woman. "For God knows that when

you eat of it your eyes will be opened, and you will be like God, knowing good and evil." (Genesis 3:1-5)

Lucifer approached Eve in much the same manner he approaches us today. He asked a simple question that cast doubt on the character and intentions of God. He begins with an exaggeration that makes Jehovah look like a real killjoy: "You mean to tell me that your Creator won't let you eat from any of these gorgeous fruit trees? That's brutal!" Satan knew that Eve would defend God at this point by clarifying the issue: "Oh, it's not so bad. You see, we can eat from every tree but that one right there in the middle."

The trap was set. Now he could move in for the kill by insinuating that God was lying just to put limitations on their happiness and fulfillment: "You're not going to die! The Creator knows full well that you will quickly jump to His level if you can just get a bite of that fruit from the tree in the middle." So Eve went first, and then Adam. As the old saying goes, "It wasn't the apple on the tree, it was the pair on the ground!"

In our day, the devil may ask questions like, "Did God really say that you couldn't have sex with someone other than your spouse? Get real! God knows that when you have that extramarital affair, you will experience pleasures you didn't even know existed! He's just trying to ruin your fun!"

"Did God really say that you shouldn't cheat on your income taxes? Wait a minute! The government is so corrupt that they will just use that money for their own evil purposes anyway. Keep more of your money for yourself! God knows how the system works."

"Do you really think the Lord was serious when He said that we shouldn't step on others in order to get to the top? Who is He kidding?! It's the only way to get ahead in the business world! Don't worry about someone else's feelings—just do what you have to do to be the winner!"

Incidentally, this may be the best way to tell the difference between the voice of the Lord and the voice of the devil. Christ speaks to us through statements and directives. Satan, the notorious "accuser of our brothers" (Revelation 12:10), seeks to cast doubt by asking questions. And his questions are always loaded in the direction of temptation.

Paul describes our battle with the tempter:

> Finally, be strong in the Lord and in his mighty power. Put on the full armor of God so that you can take your stand against the devil's schemes. For our struggle is not against flesh and blood, but against the rulers, against the authorities, against the powers of this dark

world and against the spiritual forces of evil in
the heavenly realms. Therefore, put on the full
armor of God. . . . (Ephesians 6:10-13a)

The word translated "schemes" here could be
paraphrased as "tricky ways." Indeed, the enemy of
our souls comes armed and dangerous with numerous beguiling tactics and techniques. Though sometimes revealed as a "roaring lion" (1 Peter 5:8), he
can also come to us as "an angel of light" (2 Corinthians 11:14). No doubt Eve assumed he was the latter
as she conversed with him in the Garden of Eden.

THE SINFUL NATURE

Third, temptation comes from the sinful nature. Both Paul and James completely exonerate
God in the process of temptation. And they both
point to the most common culprit. Here is a description of the source for most of our temptation:

> So I find this law at work: When I want to
> do good, evil is right there with me. For in my
> inner being I delight in God's law; but I see
> another law at work in the members of my
> body, waging war against the law of my mind
> and making me a prisoner of the law of sin at
> work within my members. (Romans 7:21-23)

> . . . each one is tempted when, by his own
> evil desire, he is dragged away and enticed.

Then, after desire has conceived, it gives birth to sin; and sin, when it is full-grown, gives birth to death. (James 1:14-15)

The "evil desire" which James describes at the front end of sin's cycle comes from this "law of sin" portrayed by Paul. Other nicknames would be "the flesh," "the carnal nature," "the old man," "the old nature" and "the Adamic nature." It is a reference to that inner urge to follow the dictates of our fallen human nature. And without exception, all of us are subject to its presence in our lives. This is the greatest source of our temptation.

THE SIN CYCLE

I have been referring to "the sin cycle," and now it is time to define it. It is a process that begins with temptation and ends in the death that sin produces. The passage I quoted above from James outlines the pattern of this cycle:

STAGE 1

WE ARE TEMPTED BY OUR OWN EVIL DESIRE

It could start when we see a beautiful woman or a handsome man walk by. Perhaps a glance at an unattended cash register drawer which is open. Maybe angry words are forming in your mind as you think about what you may want to say to someone who

has offended you. Whatever triggers that old nature that is within us becomes Stage 1 of the sin cycle.

STAGE 2

WE BEGIN TO COMPROMISE OUR CONSCIENCE

James calls this being "dragged away and enticed." Our will begins to break down as we contemplate the sinful deed that has been stimulated by the carnal nature. This is the point at which we are "mulling over" the possibility of sinning. We haven't acted on the impulse yet, but the stage is set to do so. We have, however, been impregnated with the idea.

STAGE 3

WE COMMIT THE ACT OF SIN

"After desire has conceived, it gives birth to sin." The pregnancy goes full term and the result is the birth of a sinful act. The "child" that is conceived by lust will always have the same name: sin. Nothing else can be produced by the union of evil desire and our fallen nature.

STAGE 4

WE EXPERIENCE THE DEATH TO WHICH SIN GIVES BIRTH

"Sin, when it is full-grown, gives birth to death." The child of lust is sin, and the grandchild is death.

This is true because sin has its own "life-cycle," and the end result is always the same. We see this in both the Old and New Testaments: "The soul who sins is the one who will die" (Ezekiel 18:4); "For the wages of sin is death" (Romans 6:23).

To illustrate the sin cycle in all four stages, consider a married man who is tempted to commit adultery. He thinks about a certain married woman for a long time and eventually decides to find out if she might also have an interest in him. It turns out that she, too, is willing to break her vows and so they have an affair. The end result of this sin is death. It may be the "death" of the marriages out of which both people came. It could be the "death" that is produced in the hearts of children when parents get divorced. Ultimately, if the adultery is not confessed and forsaken, it will mean eternal death: "For of this you can be sure: No immoral, impure or greedy person . . . has any inheritance in the kingdom of Christ and of God." (Ephesians 5:5)

The sin cycle is not on my list of "pleasant things to talk about." But it is very real, and we must acknowledge our place in this process. Are we at Stage 1? Have we progressed to Stages 2 and 3? Perhaps we are suffering the consequences of Stage 4. But regardless of where we may find ourselves in the temptation continuum, there is good news: Just as we can expect temptation, we can expect deliverance!

BREAKING THE STRONG-HOLD OF TEMPTATION

Though God is not the source of our temptation, He is the source of our victory over it, and He will use the experience to strengthen us. As we seek to break the stronghold of temptation, Peter offers us this blessed assurance: "His divine power has given us everything we need for life and godliness . . ." (2 Peter 1:3).

The apostle Paul exudes hope in this classic passage from First Corinthians: "No temptation has seized you except what is common to man. And God is faithful; he will not let you be tempted beyond what you can bear. But when you are tempted, he will also provide a way out so that you can stand up under it" (10:13).

Just as we can expect the experience of temptation to be "common," we can also expect God to be "faithful." Paul tells us that our Lord will never "overload the circuits." He will provide "a way out." This does not always mean that the temptation itself will simply "go away." Rather, we will be given strength to "stand up under it."

Some Christians seem to be striving to reach a level of Christianity where there will be no more temptation at all. They seek to be "dead" to any and every sinful impulse. But this is not only an unreal expectation, it is an unbiblical one. This is the key to Romans 6:6: "For

we know that our old self was crucified with him so that the body of sin might be done away with, that we should no longer be slaves to sin. . . ."

The phrase "done away with" ("destroyed," KJV) actually means "rendered powerless." The carnal nature is "done away with" or "destroyed" only in the sense that its power to control our lives has been dismantled by Christ's death on the cross. However, that old nature will still be with us until the day we die or when Jesus returns. There is no sense in which the flesh, from which temptation arises, will be eradicated here and now.

We also tend to forget the fact that our victory over the temptations of the world, the flesh and the devil is dependent, in part, on our willingness to cooperate with the Holy Spirit. This is what Paul meant in Galatians 5:24-25: "Those who belong to Christ Jesus have crucified the sinful nature with its passions and desires. Since we live by the Spirit, let us keep in step with the Spirit."

"Keeping in step with the Spirit" means to live, moment-by-moment, in dependence on our Lord's power and grace to sustain us through the most intense kinds of temptations. We will examine this issue of spiritual triumph in much greater detail in a later chapter. But for now, we can be thankful that though we can expect temptation, we can also expect "a way out"!

CHAPTER 6

Expect Persecution

This is the tale of two pastors—Pastor A and Pastor B.

Pastor A was good with people and did a pretty good job in the pulpit. But he had one flaw in his ministry: He was not a man of his word. He failed to keep his promises and often used misleading terminology. The congregation never quite knew where he stood on any given issue. In a vain attempt to please everyone, Pastor A was always straddling the fence. This naturally brought him under a lot of criticism. "We are just being persecuted for the gospel's sake, honey," Pastor A would tell his wife. "God will make this up to us."

Pastor B also had good people skills and was a better than average preacher. One of the strengths of his ministry, however, was also a source of controversy: Pastor B never minced words. He said what he meant and meant what he said. He did so in a loving

manner, but there was a firmness about him, too. Some people didn't want to hear the unaltered truth, so they devised ways to make Pastor B's life miserable. But he knew that this just came with the territory. Jesus was persecuted; Pastor B could expect to be persecuted as well.

In this tale of two pastors, both felt they were harassed for the sake of Christ. Is that *really* what happened? Or is there a difference between the experience of Pastor A and Pastor B? The apostle Peter settles the matter:

> Dear friends, do not be surprised at the painful trial you are suffering, as though something strange were happening to you. But rejoice that you participate in the sufferings of Christ, so that you may be overjoyed when his glory is revealed. If you are insulted because of the name of Christ, you are blessed, for the Spirit of glory and of God rests on you. If you suffer, it should not be as murderer or thief, or any other kind of criminal, or even as a meddler. However, if you suffer as a Christian, do not be ashamed, but praise God that you bear that name. . . .
>
> So then, those who suffer according to God's will should commit themselves to their faithful Creator and continue to do good. (1 Peter 4:12-16, 19)

It is obvious from this passage that we can create our own persecution through carnal behavior. Pastor A fits into this category. He was not suffering "according to God's will." His painful trials were a direct result of talking out of both sides of his mouth! He could not be trusted. He was not dependable. His actions made people angry and vindictive. Pastor A can pretend that he is a partaker of the sufferings of Christ, and some people may even sympathize with him for it. But his wounds are self-inflicted.

We must be careful not to confuse genuine persecution, which results from our passion for serving God, with the counterfeit version. Many Christians are suffering today "as a meddler." They create a mess and then suffer the natural consequences. This is not what the apostle had in mind.

This is why Pastor B stands in contrast to Pastor A, according to First Peter 4. He does "participate in the sufferings of Christ" because his persecution is based on the same offenses: They both belonged to the Father's kingdom, they both told the undiluted truth and they both lived a godly life.

PERSECUTION CLARIFIED

Our Lord clarified the nature of persecution in the following passage:

> If the world hates you, keep in mind that it hated me first. If you belonged to the world, it

would love you as its own. As it is, you do not belong to the world, but I have chosen you out of the world. That is why the world hates you. Remember the words I spoke to you: "No servant is greater than his master." If they persecuted me, they will persecute you also. If they obeyed my teaching, they will obey yours also. They will treat you this way because of my name, for they do not know the One who sent me. If I had not come and spoken to them, they would not be guilty of sin. Now, however, they have no excuse for their sin. He who hates me hates my Father as well. If I had not done among them what no one else did, they would not be guilty of sin. But now they have seen these miracles, and yet they have hated both me and my Father. But this is to fulfill what is written in their Law: "They hated me without reason." (John 15:18-25)

In this teaching, Jesus explained three reasons why each of His disciples will face hatred and mistreatment:

1. WE DON'T FIT IN

First, our Master tells us that we can expect persecution because, as believers, we just don't fit in with the crowd. We belong to an entirely different spiritual family. It is sort of like wearing a green outfit to

school on the day everyone else wears red. Christians stand out in the crowd both for the things they dogmatically believe and those things they refuse to believe. We become targets for harassment both for what we do and for what we refuse to do. Because we don't "belong to the world," we are considered "aliens and strangers on earth" (Hebrews 11:13).

No one likes to be the "odd man out." This is just as true of those in the ministry as it is for those who serve the Lord in a lay capacity. Every one of us wants to "fit in" and be accepted by relatives, work associates and neighbors. But when we must choose between our relationship with Christ and anyone or anything else, there is really no choice at all. Jesus said:

> Anyone who loves his father or mother more than me is not worthy of me; anyone who loves his son or daughter more than me is not worthy of me; and anyone who does not take his cross and follow me is not worthy of me. Whoever finds his life will lose it, and whoever loses his life for my sake will find it.
>
> He who receives you receives me, and he who receives me receives the one who sent me. (Matthew 10:37-40)

We can expect harassment because of this "guilt by association." We love the things God loves, and

we hate the things God hates. This will put us at odds with those outside His kingdom. The "family of Satan" and the "family of God" have been feuding longer than the Hatfields and the McCoys, and this controversy won't end until our Lord returns to conquer the devil and his followers once and for all.

2. THE TRUTH HURTS

Second, we will be persecuted, as Christ was, for telling it like it is. "If I had not come and spoken to them, they would not be guilty of sin" (John 15:22). Jesus told the truth, the whole truth, and nothing but the truth. But it got Him into big trouble—especially with the religious establishment of His day. The Savior uncloaked sin, and He started with the spiritual leaders.

It should not be completely shocking to discover that the driving force behind the execution of Jesus Christ was a group made up primarily of chief priests, scribes and elders. These men wanted Him dead because He dared to castigate them for their pride and hypocrisy. The truth that set many people free infuriated the religious hierarchy.

We, too, will feel the pinch of this reality. When we tell the truth and live the truth, some will take offense. This does not have to take place from a pulpit. Our commitment to integrity will

When they hurled their insults at him, he did not retaliate; when he suffered, he made no threats. Instead, he entrusted himself to him who judges justly. (1 Peter 2:21-23)

Blessed are those who are persecuted because of righteousness, for theirs is the kingdom of heaven.

Blessed are you when people insult you, persecute you and falsely say all kinds of evil against you because of me. Rejoice and be glad, because great is your reward in heaven, for in the same way they persecuted the prophets who were before you. (Matthew 5:10-12)

You have heard that it was said, "Love your neighbor and hate your enemy." But I tell you: Love your enemies and pray for those who persecute you. (5:43-44)

When we are cursed, we bless; when we are persecuted, we endure it; when we are slandered, we answer kindly. (1 Corinthians 4:12-13)

Bless those who persecute you; bless and do not curse. (Romans 12:14)

The theme of these passages may appear to be "Pacifists of the World, Unite!" But this is not really the point at all. Jesus does not call us to a passive response to persecution and its perpetrators. Instead we are called to an aggressive posture of acceptance, joy and appropriate response.

First, we respond with acceptance because persecution is to be expected. "To this you were called, because Christ suffered for you, leaving you an example, that you should follow in his steps" (1 Peter 2:21). Jesus was misunderstood and mistreated almost from His first day of public ministry. Throughout His three-and-one-half years of service, He suffered. Then Christ experienced the ultimate persecution in becoming the sacrifice for the sin of the whole world. The one and only time He called His Father "God" was during that dark moment on the cross when He faced His first separation from the Father because of our iniquity: "My God, my God, why have you forsaken me?" (Matthew 27:46).

The Old Testament prophets and saints were persecuted. The early church leaders and members were the victims of frequent harassment, scourging, mocking, court trials, imprisonments, and martyrdom. *Foxe's Book of Martyrs* chronicles the unbelievable suffering of many great saints in the past five centuries. And though we are blessed with a minimal amount of persecution today, we do need to accept the fact that we will suffer to some degree for our faith in Christ. I personally believe that evangelical Christians may once again face terrible suffering in the near future.

We have been "called" to persecution. We should just accept it. This is why we should follow our Lord's example by entrusting ourselves to Him who judges justly (1 Peter 2:23). God will take care of us even as He took care of His one and only Son. He is keeping all the records, and not one thing slips by Him unnoticed. Our Lord is utterly trustworthy. Unlike earthly referees and umpires, He will never miss a play or make a bad call.

Second, we can respond with joy because we are in good company and we will be rewarded: ". . . in the same way they persecuted the prophets who were before you" (Matthew 5:12). It should bring joy to our hearts to know that we do not suffer alone. The writer of Hebrews reviews some of the people in God's "Hall of Fame," and then exhorts us to rejoice in such good company:

> Others were tortured. . . . Some faced jeers and flogging, while still others were chained and put in prison. They were stoned; they were sawed in two; they were put to death by the sword . . . destitute, persecuted and mistreated—the world was not worthy of them. They wandered in deserts and mountains, and in caves and holes in the ground. . . .
>
> Therefore, since we are surrounded by such a great cloud of witnesses, let us throw off everything that hinders and the sin that so easily

entangles, and let us run with perseverance the race marked out for us. Let us fix our eyes on Jesus, the author and perfecter of our faith, who for the joy set before him endured the cross, scorning its shame, and sat down at the right hand of the throne of God. Consider him who endured such opposition from sinful men, so that you will not grow weary and lose heart. (Hebrews 11:35-38; 12:1-3)

Note that it was for "the joy set before Him" that Jesus took hell in our place. It was the exhilaration of knowing that He was providing a way for each and every human being to be reconciled with God. Our joy in persecution is based on the fact that we are privileged to share in some small way in the sufferings of our Savior and all the other saints who have gone on before us. Thank God we are not alone! As we face hardship, we are in the company of good, godly women and men.

"Rejoice and be glad, because great is your reward in heaven" (Matthew 5:12). This is the other side of the joy coin. We will be rewarded for our patience and perseverance. All of the arguments made on Christ's behalf. Sleepless nights because of some conflict caused by our Christian faith. The stress of a divided family for Jesus' sake. In the words of the old gospel song, "It will be worth it all when we see Jesus."

Third, we respond appropriately because of Christ Who lives in us. The following reactions are rather remarkable:

"He did not retaliate" (1 Peter 2:23).

"He made no threats" (1 Peter 2:23).

"Love your enemies" (Matthew 5:44).

"Pray for those who persecute you" (Matthew 5:44).

"When . . . cursed, we bless" (1 Corinthians 4:12).

"When . . . slandered, we answer kindly" (1 Corinthians 4:13).

Not only are these responses remarkable, they are absolutely impossible, but for the power of the indwelling Christ. Our first inclination is to retaliate, threaten, hate, pray against our persecutors and curse or slander them! This is an understandable reaction to mistreatment.

However, we are called to love and pray for the perpetrators. We are to bless them and respond kindly to them. Once we acknowledge the fact that we cannot react this way through our own strength or virtue, we can put our complete trust in the Lord Jesus to love our enemies through us. The Savior is the only One who was ever able to treat His persecutors with kindness. While hanging on the cross after being humiliated in every possible way, our Lord said, "Father, forgive them, for they do not know what they are doing" (Luke 23:34).

This same Jesus lives in your heart and mine. When Paul used the phrase "Christ in you, the hope of glory" (Colossians 1:27), he was referring to the reality that the Savior can live His life through us. If we will deny ourselves and put our faith in Him, He will respond appropriately in our place. "I have been crucified with Christ and I no longer live, but Christ lives in me. The life I live in the body, I live by faith in the Son of God, who loved me and gave himself for me" (Galatians 2:20).

Relying on our own ability to forgive, love and bless those who persecute us will lead only to frustration. Only Jesus can do this in and through us.

Have you been caught off guard by persecution? Did you think that when you gave your heart to Jesus Christ that everyone around you would approve? This was not the case for the many Christians who have gone before us. And though the Savior does not guarantee that we will escape tribulations, He does promise to be with us every step of the way. Ultimately, we can expect deliverance from all persecution on a permanent basis! "It will be worth it all when we see Jesus."

CHAPTER 7

Expect Doubts

Jim was a missionary among tribal people in Irian Jaya, Indonesia. The work was extremely difficult, and conversions to Christ were rare. But one day something happened that changed all of that.

Suspicions were growing among the tribesman as to the power of this God that Jim claimed to represent. The people had their own form of religion built around special idols and witch doctors. Was there any real difference between the gods they worshiped and the God of the missionary? How could anyone know that difference if there was one?

As Jim prayed one day, the Lord gave him a rather radical idea. He was instructed to call together the witch doctors and priests from the tribe. Two large piles of wood would be placed in the middle of a field on the top of a nearby mountain. There would then be a "showdown" between the God of the Bible and the gods of the tribespeople. Both would have an opportunity to pray to their deity and request fire to fall and burn the wood. The two sides agreed ahead of time that the God who answered by fire would in fact be the "real God." The date for the showdown was set.

When that day arrived, a much larger crowd gathered than the one that had been anticipated. The word had spread concerning the confrontation that would take place, and people from many tribes were curious about the outcome. They journeyed from many miles around to reach this mountain where the God of the missionary would face off with the gods of the tribespeople.

The witch doctors went first. Starting at 9 A.M., they prayed and they danced. Then they screamed and danced even more energetically. By noon, nothing had happened, and Jim began to taunt them: "Maybe you should shout a little louder! Perhaps your god is thinking about something else right now. Too busy? Traveling and cannot be reached for comment? Wait a minute—I know—he's taking a nap!"

This infuriated the witch doctors. It only made them more determined to get an answer from their god. So they cranked up the volume to the next level. They began to cut themselves as a display of their intensity. Blood flowed freely down their chests and legs. But by the evening, there was still no response. No answer. No one paid attention.

At dusk, it was Jim's turn.

So confident was this dear brother in his God that he asked some friends to dig a trench around the woodpile and pour twelve barrels of water over it. After it had been thoroughly soaked, he offered this simple prayer: "Lord, I want these people to know that You are the true and only God. Please answer my prayer by sending fire to burn up this pile of wood. Do it for Your glory. Thank you."

Even before the words "thank you" passed over Jim's lips, a ball of fire raced from the sky and exploded onto the wood. The light from this blaze was so intense that the entire sky appeared to be glowing for miles. The combustion created an inferno that vaporized the wet wood and the considerable water in the trenches around it. The ground wasn't even damp when the smoke cleared.

The reaction of the people was amazing, but understandable in these circumstances. As if in one voice, they cried out, "The missionary's God is the real God! We believe in the God of the Bible!" Thousands came to Christ in the next few days as a result of this demonstration of Jehovah's awesome power.

But the wife of the tribal chief was so angered by what she saw that she made a death threat:

"Listen to me, missionary—by this time tomorrow, you will be a dead man."

Suddenly, a deep sense of fear settled in on the missionary. For the first time in his life, he really knew what it meant to be afraid. Without giving it much thought, Jim decided to take off into the jungle. After a full day's journey, he found a nice shade tree and sat down underneath it. He just wanted to die. "I've had enough, Lord. Take my life. My faith is so weak and I just can't go back there and face that wicked woman." He laid his head down and slowly drifted off to sleep.

As you've probably figured out by now, I have modernized the story of Elijah and the showdown on Mount Carmel from First Kings 18:19-19:5. I have always marveled at the incredible contrast between the prophet we see in chapter 18 versus the one who shows up in chapter 19. How could this daring man turn into a doubting, fearful man overnight? What was so frightening about this threat from Jezebel?

We see a similar scenario unfold in the New Testament. John the Baptist was a rugged man of God. He wore hairshirts when they weren't exactly in style. John's diet consisted of a strange combination of insects and wild honey. He probably did not smell very pleasant. John proclaimed the unpopular message of repentance because, he said, "the kingdom of heaven is near" (Matthew 3:2). Here's a sample of his preaching:

> You brood of vipers! Who warned you to flee from the coming wrath? Produce fruit in keeping with repentance. And do not think you can say to yourselves, "We have Abraham as our father." I tell you that out of these stones God can raise up children for Abraham. The ax is already at the root of the trees, and every tree that does not produce good fruit will be cut down and thrown into the fire. (3:7-10)

John the Baptist was also famous for his denunciation of the illicit relationship between Herod and his brother's wife, Herodius. The prophet openly condemned the king's immorality: "It is not lawful for you to have her" (14:4). Herod had John arrested for this and thrown into prison. In a gruesome development, he was later beheaded because of the king's foolish promise made to the daughter of Herodius in a lustful moment (14:6-11).

But John the Baptist is known best as God's "master of ceremonies" to introduce Jesus Christ and His kingdom to the world for the very first time. It was a dramatic role, and one that was reserved for only the most humble, sincere follower of God. His carefully chosen words reflect on his subservience to his Master:

I baptize you with water for repentance. But after me will come one who is more powerful than I, whose sandals I am not fit to carry. He will baptize you with the Holy Spirit and with fire. His winnowing fork is in his hand, and he will clear his threshing floor, gathering his wheat into the barn and burning up the chaff with unquenchable fire. (3:11-12)

John the Baptist was a man who clearly understood his role. He knew exactly who Christ was, and that he had been appointed to introduce Him. John could be described in many ways, but after reading the early accounts of the Gospel writers, no one would think to label this great man as a "doubter." This is precisely why Matthew 11 comes as such a shock: "When John heard in prison what Christ was doing, he sent his disciples to ask him, 'Are you the one who was to come, or should we expect someone else?'" (11:2-3).

Could this possibly be the same man who introduced the Savior to the world in Matthew 3? How could such a courageous man who once stood up to the king himself get tangled in a whirlpool of uncertainty? There seem to be some similarities between what we read here and the experience that Elijah went through after the great victory on Mount Carmel. Indeed, the stories of Elijah and

John the Baptist offer several lessons with regard to our common struggle with doubt.

THE DOUBTING THOMAS IN EACH OF US

"Doubting Thomas" got his nickname from the postresurrection story in John's Gospel:

> A week later his disciples were in the house again, and Thomas was with them. Though the doors were locked, Jesus came and stood among them and said, "Peace be with you!" Then he said to Thomas, "Put your finger here; see my hands. Reach out your hand and put it into my side. Stop doubting and believe."
>
> Thomas said to him, "My Lord and my God!" (John 20:26-28)

The skeptical spirit of Thomas dwells within each of us to varying degrees. The predisposition for doubting is common to every Christian. I think the Holy Spirit included stories of great men and women of God who struggled to believe for a very simple reason: He wanted us to know that all of us can expect a certain amount of doubt as we walk with God.

I remember being amazed when my father first shared with me about a deep depression he experienced early in his ministry. Over a three-week period, he wrestled with the most basic questions about

God's existence, the creation of the world and the meaning of life. He talked about the tremendous guilt he felt because he was a minister, and ministers are not supposed to have doubts—they are expected to help others with their unbelief.

I'm not so astonished as I think about my dad's testimony now. You see, I've had my own detours with doubt. Some of them have been intense. As I have spoken candidly with colleagues in the ministry, without exception these men and women know what it feels like to struggle with unbelief. The frequency and severity of those doubts will vary from person to person. But no one I know denies the reality of a wavering faith.

SOURCES OF DOUBT

Doubt can be the result of a number of factors.

1. STRESS CAN LEAD TO UNBELIEF

Consider the background of the stories we've looked at thus far. Elijah followed up the emotional showdown on Mount Carmel by outrunning Ahab's chariot to Jezreel. He was so exhausted from all his running and Jezebel's death threat that he collapsed under a broom tree and fell asleep. To say that Elijah was "stressed out" is a huge understatement.

John the Baptist knew that he was placed in prison to die because he had dared to condemn the king's wickedness. Herod was only looking for a good excuse to kill him. John would have been executed sooner except for the fact that the king knew that this prophet was revered by the people. During those weeks and months of waiting on death row, John could envision that day when the guards would come for him. How long before he breathed his last breath on this earth? How would he be killed? These are the kinds of questions that set a person up for despair and doubt.

Thomas had just been through several days of hiding with the other disciples. His Master had been brutally murdered, and those who followed this Messiah would probably be next. Tensions were high as they met together after the crucifixion. Thomas may have wondered if he was just "seeing things" when Christ suddenly appeared without even entering through the door! "Maybe I'm just seeing Jesus here in the room because I want to see Him here so badly! I need the Savior now more than ever!"

My father's battle with doubt came on the heels of an extended time of prayer and fasting. Physically, he was very weak. Anyone who has fasted for more than a few days knows that an empty stomach can play games with the mind.

Do you see the common thread here? During times of stress, we are the most vulnerable to doubt. God does not remove our human emotions when we are saved. We are still susceptible to emotional weakness when we become physically drained by intense circumstances—especially those that are beyond our control. Just knowing this fact about our makeup as flesh-and-blood creatures can assist us in our struggle with unbelief. In this sense, it is important for us to be in tune with our bodies so that we can be aware of those times when we might have a stronger tendency to doubt.

2. SATAN CAN STIR UP DOUBT

In his very first recorded conversation, Satan revealed one of his favorite tactics: developing doubt which leads to defeat: "Did God really say, 'You must not eat from any tree in the garden'?" (Genesis 3:1).

In this case, he wanted Eve to question the character and intentions of God. But he won't stop there. The devil will plant seeds of doubt in our minds about our salvation, the forgiveness of our sins, the reality of eternal life in heaven, the veracity of the Scriptures and other basic tenets of our faith. He is aware of the fact that this can lead to deep despair. This kind of doubt can suck the joy right out of our Christian walk.

We need to recognize this tactic of our soul's greatest enemy. Lucifer will do anything and everything in his power to discourage and defeat us through insinuation. He is well aware of the powerful effect which doubt can have in our lives. Even though he cannot ultimately harm those who are in Christ, Satan will try to make life as miserable as possible for us to diminish our effectiveness. He is as crafty as he is cruel.

3. SIN CAN LEAD TO DOUBT

Another factor in our struggle with unbelief can be unconfessed sin. If we become trapped in sinful habits, it will form a cloud of doubt and despair over everything we do. The psalmist shares some pertinent thoughts on this issue:

> Blessed is he
>> whose transgressions are forgiven,
>> whose sins are covered.
> Blessed is the man
>> whose sin the LORD does not count
>>> against him
>> and in whose spirit is no deceit.
>
> When I kept silent,
>> my bones wasted away

through my groaning all day long.
For day and night
    your hand was heavy upon me;
my strength was sapped
    as in the heat of summer.
Then I acknowledged my sin to you
    and did not cover up my iniquity.
I said, "I will confess
    my transgressions to the LORD"—
and you forgave
    the guilt of my sin. . . .

If I had cherished sin in my heart,
    the LORD would not have listened;
but God has surely listened
    and heard my voice in prayer.
(Psalm 32:1-5; 66:18-19)

Unconfessed sin in our lives creates quite a stir.
Nothing is as it should be until we confess and forsake our iniquity. There are physical, emotional,
mental and spiritual consequences unless the matter
gets settled. Our prayers will go unanswered until
we offer the one supplication that God has been
waiting to hear: the prayer of confession.

It is easy to see how such spiritual vacillation plays
havoc on our faith. If we insist on living a double
life—harboring known sin while trying to walk with
God—we will experience many forms of unbelief.
James warns that the "double-minded" person is

"unstable in all he does" (James 1:8). We could call this "self-imposed doubt," or perhaps, more accurately, "sin-imposed doubt."

If we are involved in sin, we should not be surprised that we find it difficult to become grounded in our faith. This is a natural result of reaping doubt where we have sown sin. However, the moment we truly walk away from that transgression, our faith is restored and our doubt is removed.

4. SKEPTICISM WILL LEAD TO DOUBT

We live in a world that demands proof "beyond a reasonable doubt." Many people seem to have a chip on their shoulder that says, "Oh yeah? Prove it!" We demand evidence, reasons and explanations. In a word, we are taught to be skeptical about everything.

Of course, this is what got "Doubting Thomas" into trouble. He just had to have undeniable proof of Christ's resurrected body before he could believe. Our Lord's rebuke to Thomas is important for us to remember in this scientific age: "Because you have seen me, you have believed; blessed are those who have not seen and yet have believed" (John 20:29).

If we give in to the skepticism of our society, doubt can be an immovable mountain in our lives. Faith is "being sure of what we hope for and certain of what we do not see," according to Hebrews

11:1. And without it, "it is impossible to please God" (11:6). Thus it becomes a crucial factor in our maturation as a Christian. If we are going to grow in Christ, we must get beyond the scientific method. We must move past what we can see, feel, hear, smell and taste. God invites us into another dimension—the dimension of faith.

DEALING WITH DOUBT

During the writing of this book, a dear friend of mine in the ministry lost his father due to a severe lung infection. His dad was a preacher too and they were very close. Shortly after his death, my friend was haunted by doubts about his father's whereabouts. "What if none of this is real, and my dad just simply ceased to exist? What if he just got lost out in the vast universe?" Both Satan and stress were toying with his mind. But his wife reminded him of the beautiful promise in Psalm 139:

> Where can I go from your Spirit?
>   Where can I flee from your presence?
> If I go up to the heavens, you are there;
>   if I make my bed in the depths, you are
>   there.
> If I rise on the wings of the dawn,
>   if I settle on the far side of the sea,
> even there your hand will guide me,

your right hand will hold me fast.
(Psalm 139:7-10)

My friend was relieved of his doubt when he was reminded by Scripture that his father was, in the words of the old hymn, "safe in the arms of Jesus." And this is a beautiful illustration of how we must deal with a wavering faith. We must get back to God's Word, because "Faith comes from hearing the message, and the message is heard through the word of Christ" (Romans 10:17).

The Bible was given to us to build our faith. John put it this way:

> Jesus did many other miraculous signs in the presence of his disciples, which are not recorded in this book. But these are written that you may believe that Jesus is the Christ, the Son of God, and that by believing, you may have life in his name. (John 20:30-31)

Though we can expect times of doubt for each and every believer, the way back to faith will always be through God's Word. It may sound simplistic, but the old saying is true nonetheless: "God said it; I believe it; that settles it!" Some doubts may linger, and we may need to go back to the Bible on several occasions over a period of time. But eventually His Word will dispel the uncertainty, and we will stand once again on firm ground.

This is why it is important to discipline ourselves in devotions and get daily exposure to the Bible. Scripture memory becomes vital ammunition to fight off the trickery of doubt. As we give ourselves to the study of God's Word, our confidence increases while our doubtfulness decreases.

Expect doubts? Yes. They will come. But also expect this: Scripture will come to the rescue every time.

CHAPTER 8

Expect Growth

When my daughter Andrea finally got her driver's license, I had tears of joy in my eyes. She sailed easily through driver's education classes and passed the written permit test twice with flying colors. (She had to take it a second time because she lost her first permit.) I had driven many times with her and I thought she was excellent behind the wheel.

I remember vividly how important it was for me to be able to drive. I showed up an hour early for my test the day I turned sixteen! So I knew that the consequences would be dire indeed if Andrea didn't pass the first time. Unfortunately, Minnesota had just changed the road test to make it more difficult for anyone to get their license on the first try. And she did not pass. I tried to console her the best I could, but I soon discovered that it was impossible. Andrea had to work through her own anger and sadness.

I had my own hostility issues. Evidently there are no women who administer road tests in our area. Where is "equal opportunity" when you need it the most? Most of the examiners looked downright mean—almost like they had been trained to exhibit a scowl on their faces along with a "Clint Eastwood" demeanor. It was the face of an irritated father who is about to ask, "Why were you out past your curfew?!" Teens are terrified enough about the prospect of taking the test; add an angry-looking, midlife-crisis man to the mix, and you've got real terror!

After she failed the second road test, I constructed flags just like the ones they used at the exam station. Well, almost "just like." I used fishing poles with torn-up rags waving on top, and stuck them in beverage pitchers with gravel to make them stand straight. She practiced parallel parking and corner backing while I peeked from inside the garage. Then she would let me come out and give advice for awhile. Eventually, it was "Leave me alone, dad!" after she had her fill of my considerable wisdom and talent.

The third test was very close. I spoke with the examiner after it became clear that she did not pass. "She is a good driver," he said. "She would have gotten the license today except for the fact that she didn't pull in close enough to the curb at the very end." I pleaded with him in the light of the fact that this was her third attempt. But nothing I said changed his mind. That was a tough day for both dad and daughter.

I was proud of Andrea for one very special trait I saw in her throughout this whole ordeal: she never gave up. After she got over the expected anger and frustration of failure, she got right back out there in the driveway and practiced.

My wife took Andrea for that fourth and final road test because I was in Texas on a ministry trip. I nervously called home to get the news. When I discovered she had passed the exam, I was ecstatic. I went up to a complete stranger near the pay phone and said, "This is a great day! My daughter finally passed her road test and got her driver's license!" The man looked at me a little strange, then smiled.

This was a tough trial for my sixteen-year-old. (Ditto for dad!) She was tempted to give up. Andrea felt "persecuted" by the examiners. She had doubts about whether she would ever get that driver's license. But she finally did pass, and I watched her grow through the experience of multiple failures.

The same is true in your life and mine. Chapters 4-7 may have taken on the appearance of "bad news." But we can "expect growth" because of trials, persecutions, temptations and doubts. This chapter will examine just how that happens.

GROWTH THROUGH TRIALS

The story of Joseph and his brothers (Genesis 37-50) has always fascinated me. It may have something to do with the fact that I am the youngest of five sons. I am well acquainted with sibling rivalry and all of its ramifications. There is nothing quite like the bragging younger brother to get things stirred up. Believe me—I would know!

This is exactly what happened. Jacob found it difficult not to love his baby boy more than his other sons, "because he had been born to him in his old age" (37:3). He openly demonstrated his favoritism in what we would call today a "dysfunctional family system." Jacob even went so far as to have a special, richly ornamented robe made just for Joseph. This would be like going to the mall and bringing back an expensive suit for one child and nothing for the rest of the family.

Obviously, this did not sit well with Joseph's brothers. "When his brothers saw that their father loved him more than any of them, they hated him and could not speak a kind word to him" (37:4).

Things got so out of hand that it eventually led to a discussion about the possibility of murdering the favorite son. Had not Reuben, the eldest, stepped in, Joseph would not have seen any of his dreams come true. They settled on a compromise: Sell the boy as a slave, but report him as "missing and presumed dead" to Jacob. This was accomplished by soaking Joseph's "pretty little jacket from daddy" in goat's blood. With no DNA testing available at the time, Jacob had to assume the worst: "Some ferocious animal has devoured him. Joseph has surely been torn to pieces" (37:33).

Being sold into slavery turned out to be an incredible trial of Joseph's faith. Having had visions of leadership, Jacob's youngest son must have wondered what God had in store. As if he had not been plunged deeply enough into despair, Potiphar's wife trumped up a false charge of rape when Joseph refused to have sex with her. This led to a prison sentence.

We could not have blamed Joseph for sarcastically saying to himself: "Let's see here. I've been sold into slavery. Now I've been falsely accused of raping my master's wife which is why I have been incarcerated. It sure seems like my career is right on track! How could anything else go wrong?"

But Joseph experienced incredible growth through this staggering series of trials. The proof of this shows up in Genesis 45. Because of a devastating famine, the brothers were forced to flee to Egypt and beg for food. By this time, Joseph had risen to second-in-command to Pharaoh because of his ability to interpret dreams. Here's the remarkable scene:

So there was no one with Joseph when he made himself known to his brothers. And he wept so loudly that the Egyptians heard him, and Pharaoh's household heard about it.

Joseph said to his brothers, "I am Joseph! Is my father still living?" But his brothers were not able to answer him, because they were terrified at his presence.

Then Joseph said to his brothers, "Come close to me." When they had done so, he said, "I am your brother Joseph, the one you sold into Egypt! And now, do not be distressed and do not be angry with yourselves for selling me here, because it was to save lives that God sent me ahead of you . . . to preserve for you a remnant on earth and to save your lives by a great deliverance.

So then, it was not you who sent me here, but God. . . .

You intended to harm me, but God intended it for good. . . ." (45:1-5, 7-8; 50:20)

Joseph's brothers must have thought they were having a nightmare when he revealed his true identity! How does one go from slavery to royalty? It seemed impossible that he could be standing before them. But then reality set in. They must have had some interesting thoughts before Joseph demonstrated his grace and mercy. "Little Joe certainly has us where he wants us. What kind of revenge will he want? We're dead! There's no hope! He has every right to order our immediate executions!"

But little did they know just how much "growing up" their youngest brother had experienced through the trials of the past few years. He was not even the slightest bit vindictive. He had caught a vision of God's "big picture." Something that looked totally wrong and bad turned out to be thoroughly right and good. The measure of Joseph's personal growth becomes evident in his demonstration of mercy toward brothers who deserved to be punished. Had he not walked through those deep waters, he would not have been able to exhibit such grace under pressure.

In a humorous and human aside, Joseph gave this instruction to his brothers as they returned to get Jacob and the moving van: "Don't quarrel on the way!" (45:24). For all of his growth, there was still a bossy little brother inside. Is this a great story or what?

GROWTH THROUGH TEMPTATIONS

There is a lot of conjecture as to what constituted Paul's "thorn in the flesh." Listen to his description of the struggle:

> To keep me from becoming conceited because of these surpassingly great revelations,

there was given me a thorn in my flesh, a messenger of Satan, to torment me. Three times I pleaded with the Lord to take it away from me. But he said to me, "My grace is sufficient for you, for my power is made perfect in weakness." Therefore I will boast all the more gladly about my weaknesses, so that Christ's power may rest on me. That is why, for Christ's sake, I delight in weaknesses, in insults, in hardships, in persecutions, in difficulties. For when I am weak, then I am strong. (2 Corinthians 12:7-10)

My personal opinion is that Paul's "thorn in the flesh" was a recurring temptation to commit a particular sin. Like all of us, the apostle wanted complete deliverance from the very allure of evil. But God would not grant this because he wanted Paul, as He wants us, to be completely dependent on Him. If the possibility of temptation was completely removed from us, we would have an even greater problem with pride. Remember, this passage started with the words, "To keep me from becoming conceited . . ."

Paul could testify that he experienced spiritual growth through this repeated battle with temptation. This struggle put him in a place of humble subordination to his Lord and Master. He would never feel like he had "arrived" or that he was better than other Christians. That kind of meekness is truly a sign of spiritual maturity. Indeed, Paul meant it when he said, "I am less than the least of all God's people" (Ephesians 3:8).

We looked at First Corinthians 10:13 in chapter 5. The phrase at the end is a reference to the kind of growth that we can expect from our frequent bouts with temptation: "But when you are tempted, he will also provide a way out so that you can stand up under it."

The words "stand up under it" evoke the image of the weightlifter competing in what is called the "clean-and-jerk." He quickly raises the barbell over his head and then sustains that weight by moving his feet from front to back in a scissorlike fashion. In this way, the weightlifter "stands up under it." An obvious result of this maneuver is that the competitors will be able to "stand up under" greater amounts of weight as their muscles gain strength from each lift.

So it is in your life and mine. We will be able to manage larger enticements to evil as we conquer the smaller ones. This is all part of the growth process which takes place through the auspices of temptation. Though God cannot be accused of creating the allurement to evil, He can use our weakness to show us His strength. We can become wonderfully stripped of self-confidence as we face those temptations that we cannot overcome on our own. This is growth.

GROWTH THROUGH PERSECUTION

In the parable of the sower, Jesus warned about how persecution can expose the fickleness and immaturity of the ungrounded believer:

> The one who received the seed that fell on rocky places is the man who hears the word and at once receives it with joy. But since he has no root, he lasts only a short time. When trouble or persecution comes because of the word, he quickly falls away" (Matthew 13:20-21).

For those who have no root, persecution weakens them all the more.

Fortunately, the opposite is true, too—persecution strengthens the grounded believer. Paul says:

> But we have this treasure in jars of clay to show that this all-surpassing power is from God and not from us. We are hard pressed on every side, but not crushed; perplexed, but not in despair; persecuted, but not abandoned; struck down, but not destroyed. . . .
>
> Therefore, we do not lose heart. Though outwardly we are wasting away, yet inwardly we are being renewed day by day. For our

light and momentary troubles are achieving for us an eternal glory that far outweighs them all. So we fix our eyes not on what is seen, but on what is unseen. For what is seen is temporary, but what is unseen is eternal. (2 Corinthians 4:7-9; 16-18)

Where it counts the most—internally—we can expect growth as a pay-off for persecution. These verses speak of a depth in the disciples' character that only suffering can produce. They had shifted their attention away from the temporal scene here on earth and were focused on what these short years would mean for all eternity. And they very much liked that vision of the future.

Early in the book of Acts are two illustrations of spiritual growth as a direct consequence of persecution. The first involves the apostles:

The apostles left the Sanhedrin, rejoicing because they had been counted worthy of suffering disgrace for the Name. Day after day, in the temple courts and from house to house, they never stopped teaching and proclaiming the good news that Jesus is the Christ" (5:41-42).

Note that there is none of the typical "Why me?" response to suffering. These men felt highly privileged to be persecuted for the Savior. As evidence of their growth through these experiences, they became even more bold in their proclamation of the gospel.

Then there's the story of Stephen, who paid the ultimate price for following His Lord: martyrdom.

> . . . yelling at the top of their voices, they all rushed at him, dragged him out of the city and began to stone him. . . .
>
> While they were stoning him, Stephen prayed, "Lord Jesus, receive my spirit." Then he fell on his knees and cried out, "Lord, do not hold this sin against them." When he had said this, he fell asleep. (7:57-60)

Just like Joseph and Jesus, Stephen did not want his persecutors to get what they deserved. His last request was for the pardon of those who were pummeling his body with stones. Is this not a man who demonstrates remarkable depth of character and spiritual growth because of his persecution?

Few would challenge the notion that Christians today, particularly North American believers, are generally far more immature than those in centuries past. There may be a very simple explanation for this phenomenon: The modern church in the United States and Canada has not faced any serious degree of persecution. Conditions have been conducive to becoming spiritually soft and pudgy.

In countries where the church has experienced persecution (Russia, China and Vietnam, to name a few), we see a corresponding maturity and depth of character that only suffering can produce. Does this mean that we should *pray for* persecution, so that we can grow up? No. But we need to be diligent in our efforts to overcome the inertia of the peaceful times in which we live. It is more difficult to grow during good times.

Will this calm last? Probably not. I am inclined to believe that the church of Jesus Christ will face some very difficult days prior to His second coming. But whether or not that happens, we must trust the Lord to use even our "momentary and light afflictions" to produce growth for our walk with Christ.

GROWTH THROUGH DOUBTS

Doubts have a tendency to make us dig. And when we are forced to truly dig for answers, the result is a sense of solid reassurance.

The author of Psalm 73 struggled with haunting doubts about what he called the "prosperity of the wicked." He observed that *sinners* are often the ones who seem to have the money and the health to enjoy it. Is there a Christian anywhere who has not been perplexed by this troubling reality? Missionaries are forced to come home from eternally important ministries overseas because of a life-threatening cancer while peddlers of pornography don't even seem to catch a cold! "Their bodies are healthy and strong. . . . The wicked are . . . always carefree, they increase in wealth" (73:4, 12). How can this possibly be fair or just?

This led the psalmist to frankly confess that he "nearly lost his foothold" (73:2) because of this line of thinking. "Surely in vain have I kept my heart pure" (73:13). Haven't you ever felt this way? I certainly have! What's the use of going all out for Jesus if sinners win in the long run?

But right there is the catch!

> When I tried to understand all this,
>   it was oppressive to me
> till I entered the sanctuary of God;
>   then I understood their final destiny.
>
> Surely you place them on slippery ground;
>   you cast them down to ruin.
> How suddenly are they destroyed,
>   completely swept away by terrors!
> As a dream when one awakes,
>   so when you arise, O Lord,
>   you will despise them as fantasies.
> (73:16-20)

After doing some digging, the psalmist ended up where we must all conclude when we are struggling with doubts: in the presence of God. With hearts quiet before Him, we begin to understand that this world is temporal and the world to come is eternal. It is not what we *go after here* that really matters—it's where we will *go hereafter*! We can trust God with the troubling issue of missionaries who die with cancer and sinners who prosper because of their evil deeds. Our passion must be to live for the Lord right here and right now.

My father came out of his period of doubt and depression a much stronger man of God. That friend who lost his father and wondered about his eternal state grew in the Lord because of that uncertainty. John the Baptist is able to look back at his question with a smile from his present view in paradise. I am thankful for the development I have seen in my own Christian character that resulted from those times of tough questioning.

GROWTH THROUGH A DAILY WALK

We have looked at some of the ways that growth occurs naturally through difficult circumstances. There are, of course, things we can do to enhance our own spiritual growth in our daily walk with God.

1. DAILY DEAL WITH SIN

We need to keep "short accounts" with the Lord and each other if we want to stay on the cutting edge of spiritual development. Paul states the principle clearly in Acts 24:16: "I strive always to keep my conscience clear before God and man."

Whether sins of commission (something I did that I should not have done) or omission (something I did not do that I should have done), we need to deal with each one as it comes along. We are tempted to allow that small brick of sin to multiply and become a fence, and then the fence becomes a wall. Let's expedite matters while they are still small and easier to resolve. And let's do it daily.

2. DAILY DENY THE SELF-LIFE

Some Christians are shocked to find out that when they thought they had "died to self," the old nature was really just in a "coma." We'll talk more about this in chapter 12, but the important point here is Romans 6:11: "Count yourselves dead to sin but alive to God in Christ Jesus."

A more literal translation using the present continuous verb tense from the Greek would be, "Keep on agreeing with God that the old nature has died and that you have resurrection power in Christ Jesus." We need to rely every moment of every day on the cross work of Christ to deliver us from the downward pull of the flesh. Each morning we should arise with the prayer of Galatians

2:20 in our hearts: "Lord, today I want the old nature to be crucified with You so that I can truly experience Your resurrection life and power for holy living." This will keep us on the pathway of spiritual growth.

3. DAILY DEVOTIONS FOR STRENGTH

There is simply no substitute for personal time with the Lord in prayer and Bible study. This is the spiritual nutrition that will give us spiritual health. Paul put it this way: "All Scripture is God-breathed and is useful for teaching, rebuking, correcting and training in righteousness, so that the man of God may be thoroughly equipped for every good work" (2 Timothy 3:16-17).

For evidence of our need for intimate conversation with God in prayer, look no further than to Jesus Himself. He demonstrated a dependence on His Father because of self-imposed limitations during His time on earth. His diligent prayer life is our model. We must have time with Him on a daily basis. There will be no significant spiritual growth apart from this time in the Word and with the Lord Jesus in prayer.

4. DAILY DIRECTION FOR SERVICE

Each day we need to be in tune with God to know what special plans He may have for us. It is easy to get caught up in our work and family routines to the point where we are not even open to the Holy Spirit's intervention at the moment of His choosing. There may be someone crossing our path who needs a special word of encouragement. Others could be ready to hear the gospel because of recent circumstances. Someone else might be in need of spiritual counsel which the Lord may intend to provide through you or me.

To stay on the cutting edge of growth, we need to be available throughout the day for His "marching orders." It may be a seemingly "small" matter, or something much larger than we ever dreamed. Our responsibility is simply to be faithful to listen for His direction and then follow it.

Expect growth! Sometimes it will come through trials, doubts, persecutions or temptations. And we can grow daily as we practice the disciplines of dealing with sin, denying self, finding strength in our devotions and seeking His direction for service.

CHAPTER 9

Expect Gifts

As I was growing up, there was nothing quite like the Christmas season. As one of ten children being raised in a pastor's home, I was in no danger of becoming materialistic! But our modest surroundings enabled us to enjoy the true meaning of Christ's birth without a lot of the clutter of the holidays. As a friend of mine so eloquently put it, people tend to "get trapped in the wrappings and wrapped in the trappings" of Christmas.

My father was a master of psychological games during December. Knowing that one of the kids was listening from a distance, he would say to one of his sons, "Do you think we can get Penny's present through the door, or will we need to keep it in the garage?" The word was out in a flash. Penny had at least one very large present coming on

Christmas morning! Dad had succeeded in stirring the imagination and increasing the heart rate.

When the sun finally rose on December 25, it was a mad rush to the stairs. We sat in age-order with the youngest on the bottom steps. (As the eighth child, I had the third step.) My father did his best to conduct a brief devotional to remind us of the greatest Gift that had ever been given. But we acted way too much like the children we were.

When the "Amen" was placed at the end of the prayer, we were free to run throughout the house in search of our name attached to a group of presents. The "main" gift was usually opened for us, and if it was motorized, it was up and running. Other gifts were wrapped, and we spent the next few hours taking turns opening our presents. The curiosity factor was sometimes overwhelming as we waited for the wrapping paper to be unceremoniously ripped off. And even though there was not an overabundance of money, we knew that we could expect gifts.

It was such a special day each year. I often wish I could be ten years old again for just that day—December 25—and enjoy one more childhood Christmas. Those gifts were given with love, thoughtfulness and a desire to encourage the recipient. And so it is with the gifts of the Holy Spirit. Let's look into the implications of this.

Gifts for Every Believer

Without exception, every born-again child of God will receive at least one spiritual gift. It's like Christmas in our families—no one is left out. Paul is clear on this: "Now to each one the manifestation of the Spirit is given for the common good. . . . he [the Holy Spirit] gives them to each one, just as he determines" (1 Corinthians 12:7, 11).

This is a wonderful truth in which all of us can revel. No one has been forgotten. No one has been neglected. God has chosen to freely grant each of us one or more spiritual gifts. This is true for the child who receives Christ as well as the adult who is saved late in life—and everyone in between. Lay people are gifted, as well as those called into full-time ministry. The promise is for you.

What are spiritual gifts? They are nothing more or less than supernatural enablings. It is true that to a certain extent every believer already possesses things like wisdom, knowledge, faith, discernment, etc. But those who have a spiritual gift in one of these areas will have a supernatural ability with a word of wisdom or knowledge. The man or woman with the gift of faith will have a supernatural enabling to believe God more than those of us who do not have this gift.

FEWER GIFTS, MORE HONOR

Just when we are about to complain about the fact that someone else seems to have more spiritual gifts than we do, the Word of God reminds us once again that the world in which we live thinks in an "upside-down" fashion. Our society gives greater honor to the most talented. This is not to be the case in the body of Christ.

> The eye cannot say to the hand, "I don't need you!" And the head cannot say to the feet, "I don't need you!" On the contrary, those parts of the body that seem to be weaker are indispensable, and the parts that we think are less honorable we treat with special honor. And the parts that are unpresentable are treated with special modesty, while our presentable parts need no special treatment. But God has combined the members of the body and has given greater honor to the parts that lacked it, so that there should be no division in the body, but that its parts should have equal concern for each other. If one part suffers, every part suffers with it; if one part is honored, every part rejoices with it. (12:21-26)

Paul began his exhortation on spiritual gifts in Romans 12 with these words: "Do not think of yourselves more highly than you ought, but rather think of yourself with sober judgment, in accordance with the measure of faith God has given you" (Romans 12:3).

It is so easy to become conceited because we manifest a particular spiritual gift or gifts. And if we have many supernatural enablings of the Holy Spirit, the temptation to place ourselves above other believers only increases. But we have this clear, sobering truth to face: God gives greater honor to those who have fewer gifts. This keeps the body of Christ from becoming divided, and it enables us to have "equal concern for each other" (1 Corinthians 12:25).

A lovely illustration of this truth in action can be found in Acts 6:

> In those days when the number of disciples was increasing, the Grecian Jews among them complained against the Hebraic Jews because their widows were being overlooked in the daily distribution of food. So the Twelve gathered all the disciples together and said, "It would not be right for us to neglect the ministry of the word of God in order to wait on tables. Brothers, choose seven men from among you who are known to be full of the Spirit and wisdom. We will turn this responsibility over to

them and will give our attention to prayer and the ministry of the word." (6:1-4)

Could Scripture be more practical in its application? Biblical principles can even be applied to things like food preparation and doing dishes! Rather than set themselves up as being "too big" or "too good" or "too important" to do dishes, the controversy was framed, as it should have been, in the context of spiritual gifts. Those who were ultimately selected for dish duty were considered "equals" because they, too, needed to be "full of the Spirit and wisdom." The apostles even had a special commissioning service for the kitchen crew (6:6)!

Perhaps you are feeling rather small and insignificant in the body of Christ. Your spiritual gifts are not outwardly glamorous or exciting. Let this truth sink in: God's ways are not the ways of the world. The obscure members of His family will have greater honor in His kingdom.

DIFFERENT GIFTS FOR EVERY BELIEVER

A parent will work hard to find Christmas gifts that are just right for each member of the family. And those presents would be different because every child is unique. So it is in the body of Christ. The Holy Spirit offers a variety of spiritual gifts to believers:

We have different gifts, according to the grace given us. (Romans 12:6)

There are different kinds of gifts, but the same Spirit. There are different kinds of service, but the same Lord. There are different kinds of working, but the same God works all of them in all men. (1 Corinthians 12:4-6)

They are "gifts" in the full sense of the word. We cannot earn our spiritual gifts because they are freely offered to us. It's not a matter of being good enough, naturally talented enough or intelligent enough. We receive the gifts that the Lord knows will uniquely enable us to have our maximum impact for God.

There is no hint in Scripture of a "cookie cutter" mentality, whereby all believers are to seek the same identical supernatural enablings. Our God loves variety. He chooses to do things just a little differently for each of us. It is useless to insist that everyone possess the same spiritual gift.

Now the body is not made up of one part but of many. If the foot should say, "Because I am not a hand, I do not belong to the body," it would not for that reason cease to be part of the body. . . . If the whole body were an eye, where would the sense of hearing be? If the whole body were an ear, where would the sense of smell be? But in fact God has arranged the parts in the body, every one of them, just as he wanted them to be. . . .

Are all apostles? Are all prophets? Are all teachers? Do all work miracles? Do all have gifts of healing? Do all speak in tongues? Do all interpret? (12:14-15, 17-18, 29-30)

The answer to each of those questions at the end of First Corinthians 12 is an emphatic "NO!" We are not all apostles, prophets, teachers or miracle workers. Not all of us have gifts of healing, tongues or interpretation of tongues. Why? Because God has sovereignly arranged it this way!

GIFTS SELECTED BY THE HOLY SPIRIT

I have been hinting at this, and now it is time to come right out with it: Though we can and should expect spiritual gifts when we become Christians, we should not plan on choosing them. Remember, "All these are the work of one and the same Spirit, and he gives them to each one, just as he determines" (12:11).

We are not to get caught up in a clamor over any particular spiritual gift. This is decided by the determination of the Holy Spirit alone. Many religious leaders today are misleading the flock by urging believers to seek certain gifts—especially ones that have strong emotional appeal. They teach their followers that if they do not exhibit these special enablings, it is a sign of spiritual immaturity.

But Paul proclaimed that just the opposite is true: Those who would have the audacity to challenge the wisdom of the Holy Spirit in dispersing His gifts as He sees fit are the ones who need to grow up! Our maturity is evidenced by the fact that we have submitted to the will and wisdom of God. He alone knows all about our need. He alone is aware of exactly how He intends to use us. And thus the Lord alone must decide what gift or gifts we should have to accomplish His will.

THE PURPOSE OF SPIRITUAL GIFTS

We can expect spiritual gifts to be bestowed upon us for one very special purpose: to contribute to the building of Christ's body and kingdom. Here's what the Word says:

> Just as each of us has one body with many members, and these members do not all have the same function, so in Christ we who are many form one body, and each member belongs to all the others. (Romans 12:4-5)

> Now to each one the manifestation of the Spirit is given for the common good. (1 Corinthians 12:7)

So it is with you. Since you are eager to have spiritual gifts, try to excel in gifts that build up the church. . . .

What then shall we say, brothers? When you come together, everyone has a hymn, or a word of instruction, a revelation, a tongue or an interpretation. All of these must be done for the strengthening of the church. (14:12, 26)

But to each one of us grace has been given as Christ apportioned it. This is why it says:

"When he ascended on high,
he led captives in his train
and gave gifts to men." . . .

It was he [Christ] who gave some to be apostles, some to be prophets, some to be evangelists, and some to be pastors and teachers, to prepare God's people for works of service, so that the body of Christ may be built up until we all reach unity in the faith and in the knowledge of the Son of God and become mature, attaining to the whole measure of the fullness of Christ.

Then we will no longer be infants, tossed back and forth by the waves, and blown here and there by every wind of teaching and by the cunning and craftiness of men in their deceitful scheming. Instead, speaking the truth in love, we will in all things grow up into him who is the Head, that is, Christ. From him the whole body, joined and held together by every supporting ligament, grows and builds itself up in love, as each part does its work. (Ephesians 4:7-8, 11-16).

Consider each of the key phrases from these passages that address the purpose of spiritual gifts in the life of the individual believer: "each member belongs to all the others"; "for the common good"; "for the strengthening of the church"; "to prepare God's people for works of service, so that the body of Christ may be built up."

It becomes an indisputable fact that supernatural enablings from the Holy Spirit are to help each of us serve in the body of Christ. These gifts are not for show. They are not—at least not primarily—for our own edification. We are gifted so that we can encourage, strengthen and equip others. This serves as a rebuke to anyone who would want to use a gift for selfish purposes.

DISCOVERING OUR SPIRITUAL GIFT(S)

When I was just twelve years old, I was telling everyone that I was going to be a preacher when I grew up. This was not hard for those around me to believe because I was already demonstrating communication skills beyond my years. I can remember forcing my little sisters, Pam and Penny, to participate in my version of a "church service." I say "forcing" them because this would not have been their first choice on a Saturday afternoon. Using a handwritten bulletin, I would lead them in a few songs and a prayer, take an offering and then give a sermon. Once in a while they would sneak out during prayer, so I learned to keep one eye open as I prayed.

When I entered junior high as a seventh grader, I spoke to the kids in junior church—the fourth to sixth graders. How I wish someone had made a tape recording of my messages back then! But it always came easy for me. It just seemed "natural" for Tom Allen to be up front in the role of preacher.

I continued to work on the art of public speaking by becoming a speech and communications major at Asbury College. It was there that my speech professor, a dear woman of God, took a special interest in me. Dorothy Raines spent many extra hours outside the classroom helping me hone this skill. I will never forget her contribution to my personal life and professional ministry.

It was in the summer of 1975 that my spiritual gift became evident to the body of Christ. I was a summer youth intern at my father's church in Mansfield, Ohio, and I was also active in an interdenominational Bible study for college-age students. I was asked to speak to my peers that summer and I chose a controversial subject that I felt had been avoided. I called the sermon, "The Revolutionary Principles of Christian Dating." As I gave this message, I was overwhelmed by the sense of the Holy Spirit's anointing. And for the first time ever, people wanted tapes of what I had said!

I preached for my father on a few occasions, too. At the end of that summer, I was approached by twin brothers whom God was using mightily in a revival in western Canada. Ralph and Lou Sutera took me to lunch to share with me a rather remarkable piece of information: They both felt I had the "gift of the evangelist" and asked if I would join their team in the capacity of youth speaker. By this time, I had pretty much settled the fact that I would be a pastor like my dad. So this was shocking news. But I decided to join with them and allow God to confirm this word one way or the other.

It didn't take long to realize that what the Sutera twins had discerned about me was indeed true. God used me in remarkable ways as a twenty-one-year-old evangelist that first year. My ministry exploded both nationally and internationally over the next few years. I was amazed by the way in which the Lord had chosen to use me (and so were a lot of my Sunday school teachers, who knew me when I was in grade school!).

To this day, I am keenly aware of the fact that my foremost spiritual gift is that of the evangelist. Along with that, God has granted me gifts of preaching, discernment and administration. Though I have served as a pastor at different stages in my ministry, I have never been a pastor in terms of my primary spiritual enablement.

I share this personal testimony as an example of how we can discover our spiritual gift(s). It may start as an interest or desire that we recognize in our own hearts. We may call it a "talent" at first, something that just seems to come "naturally." In my case, it was ease in front of an audience. It may only be later that we realize it is more than mere talent and is anything but natural. It is the power of the Holy Spirit working *super*naturally within us.

If it is a true spiritual gift, it will be confirmed by the body of Christ. For example, Paul said to Timothy, "Do not neglect your gift, which was given you through a prophetic message when the body of elders laid their hands on you" (1 Timothy 4:14).

It is utter foolishness to go around claiming to have this or that gift if no other spiritual leader in the body of Christ has confirmed it. We need the affirmation of the Holy Spirit and the church. Some helpful tools have been devised for those who want to discern their spiritual gift(s). I encourage you to ask the Lord to show you how He wants to use you—and then expect it to be confirmed by those who know you and love you in the body of Christ.

THE GIVER, NOT HIS GIFTS

Let me issue a simple warning as I bring this chapter to a close: Our interest in spiritual gifts must be kept in proper balance. It is a wonderful, exhilarating truth that we can expect spiritual gifts to help us do our part in Christ's body. But many today focus on the *gifts* instead of the *Giver*. In the classic hymn, "Himself," A.B. Simpson so beautifully illustrates the perspective we need to maintain:

> Once it was the blessing, Now it is the Lord;
> Once it was the feeling, Now it is His Word;
> Once His gift I wanted, Now the Giver own;
> Once I sought for healing, Now Himself
>   alone.
> All in all forever, Jesus will I sing;
> Everything in Jesus, And Jesus everything.[1]

One of the devil's greatest schemes is diversion. If he can get us to focus on spiritual gifts rather than Jesus Himself, he has won the day through this seemingly innocent diversion. Becoming wrapped up in the gifts may appear to be a mark of maturity. But when it takes us away from our worship, adoration and service for Christ, it is very immature.

Expect gifts! You are guaranteed to have at least one. God wants you to dedicate that gift for His use and His glory. And let us never allow any spiritual gift to take our focus away from the Giver Himself!

ENDNOTE

[1] A.B. Simpson, "Himself," *Hymns of the Christian Life* (Camp Hill, PA: Christian Publications, Inc., 1978), #248.

CHAPTER 10

Expect Service

As soon as they left the synagogue, they went with James and John to the home of Simon and Andrew. Simon's mother-in-law was in bed with a fever, and they told Jesus about her. So he went to her, took her hand and helped her up. The fever left her and she began to wait on them. (Mark 1:29-31)

Someone has said that there are only two ways to handle a mother-in-law—and nobody knows either of them! But in the Scripture passage above, the disciples discovered the way to handle a feverish mother-in-law: "they told Jesus about her." The result was healing for this woman. And this is good advice for any situation in our lives that is beyond our control. We must simply turn it over to our Savior. We, too, can watch God work when we surrender everything to Him.

I like the response of Simon's mother-in-law to her healing: "she began to wait on them." Because Jesus had ministered to her need, she in turn wanted to express her gratitude in the form of servanthood. She did so by preparing a meal. It was the right thing to do in the light of what Christ had just done for her. The phrase "wait on them" implies that it took a while to finish the task. Perhaps she spent several hours making a delectable dinner for the Master and His disciples.

The grace of our Lord should have the same effect on us. The forgiveness, joy and peace should stir us to servanthood. The way in which God uses trials, temptations, persecutions and doubts to accelerate our growth should enlist us into service for the Master. And the fact that the Holy Spirit has bestowed gifts upon us to be used for God's glory should also inspire active duty for the Lord. Any other response implies that we have taken these innumerable blessings for granted.

CRISIS MANAGEMENT

Someone is diagnosed with cancer; a car accident suddenly takes a person to the brink; an impending divorce is looming like a dark thundercloud. The individual caught in one of these dire circumstances rushes to make a rash and radical promise to God: "O Lord, if You'll just heal me—if You'll just spare my life—if You'll just save this marriage . . . then I promise that I will serve You for the rest of my days!"

So many times, the Lord Jesus grants these urgent requests only to be ignored when the crisis has passed. When the doctor declares that body cancer-free, when that car wreck is just a distant memory, when that marriage is mended—this is often when those solemn vows made to God are broken. "It was just an emotional time for me—that's why I made those promises." The pressure is off, and so is the promise. Many people return to the same spiritual apathy they had before tragedy struck. Clearly, this is taking advantage of God's great grace.

EMERGENCY EXITS

I travel a lot on airplanes. I like to request the "emergency exit row" because it offers more leg room for my six foot, two-inch frame. It amazes me how often we take those emergency exits for granted until they are needed. As the DC-10 I was on landed in Cleveland, Ohio, one stormy night several years ago, one of the engines was sparking and threatening to burst into flames. The flight attendant informed us of the situation by running up the aisle yelling, "Engine fire! Engine fire!" Fortunately for us, it never did become a fire. But for a moment, everyone was staring at my row—the emergency exit row!

Sometimes we treat God like that "emergency exit." He is there just in case we are facing some catastrophe, but otherwise He is ignored. We can go for days or even weeks sometimes without even so much as "saying hello" through prayer. But the moment we are in trouble of any kind, we fall on our knees and beg for help. As a sergeant in the army once wisely observed, "There are no atheists in foxholes."

A DISTORTED VIEW OF GOD

Perhaps our thinking becomes twisted because of a weak, inaccurate view of God's nature. Many want to think of God as a "kind old grandfather" who would never offend anyone. He just loves to heal us when we are sick, cheer us when we are sad and comfort us when we are scorned. He does not get too personally involved, nor does He expect anything in return. Certainly, this is the image of deity that Hollywood promotes.

But this is not, of course, a true picture of God as He is revealed in Scripture. Thankfully, Jehovah is giving, loving, merciful and full of grace. However, the realization of these facts is intended to bring us to a point of utter surrender and servanthood. To put it another way, the Creator has paid the full price for our redemption, and He intends to collect on His eternal investment in each of us.

We must not shrink back from our duty and cheapen the costly grace of Jesus Christ. He paid the total cost; we owe a total commitment. Paul looked at it this way: "I am obligated both to Greeks and non-Greeks, both to the wise and the foolish. That is why I am so eager to preach the gospel also to you who are at Rome" (Romans 1:14-15).

We are indebted to the Lord Jesus Christ for all that He has done for us. We have an obligation. We do not serve the Savior to earn our salvation, but we serve Him because He saved us! And there is a huge difference between these two statements.

A FAITH THAT WORKS

Many people today are trying to work their way to heaven by doing good works. But entrance to heaven is not granted this way. We can only share eternal bliss with the Triune God through the merits of Jesus' death and resurrection. However, this does not mean that once we are saved we can take our salvation for granted. One evidence of our new birth into the family of God is a desire to serve Him with our whole heart. Consider these passages:

> For even the Son of Man did not come to
> be served, but to serve, and to give his life as
> a ransom for many. (Mark 10:45)

For we are God's workmanship, created in Christ Jesus to do good works, which God prepared in advance for us to do. (Ephesians 2:10)

For the grace of God that brings salvation has appeared to all men. It teaches us to say "No" to ungodliness and worldly passions, and to live self-controlled, upright and godly lives in this present age, while we wait for the blessed hope—the glorious appearing of our great God and Savior, Jesus Christ, who gave himself for us to redeem us from all wickedness and to purify for himself a people that are his very own, eager to do what is good. (Titus 2:11-14)

What good is it, my brothers, if a man claims to have faith but has no deeds? Can such faith save him? Suppose a brother or sister is without clothes and daily food. If one of you says to him, "Go, I wish you well; keep warm and well fed," but does nothing about his physical needs, what good is it? In the same way, faith by itself, if not accompanied by action, is dead.

But someone will say, "You have faith; I have deeds."

Show me your faith without deeds, and I will show you my faith by what I do. . . .

As the body without the spirit is dead, so faith without deeds is dead. (James 2:14-18; 26)

Dear friends, if our hearts do not condemn us, we have confidence before God and receive from him anything we ask, because we obey his commands and do what pleases him. And this is his command: to believe in the name of his Son, Jesus Christ, and to love one another as he commanded us. Those who obey his commands live in him, and he in them. And this is how we know that he lives in us: We know it by the Spirit he gave us. (1 John 3:21-24)

The Savior Himself set the example by declaring His mission: to serve. We are created in Christ Jesus "to do good works." This is a natural development for a child of God. Grace teaches us to live a godly life and eagerly "do what is good" ("zealous of good works," Titus 2:14, KJV). James reminds us that faith must be accompanied by the validation of works. Not once does he imply that salvation can be earned by those good deeds. But exemplary behavior should be the result of genuine trust in Christ. John reminds us that our obedience and servanthood are an evidence of the fact that "He lives in us." This is the faith that works.

CHRISTIANS IN THE BLEACHERS

Saved to serve—this is the way God intended it to be. But as I look at the body of Christ these days, I am troubled by the selfishness which is so evident. Many believers do not "expect service" when they become a Christian. Some seem to embrace a philosophy that says, "saved to get more." Others hide behind the excuse that Christian service is only for those who are called to serve on a "full-time" basis.

Imagine a football team that decided to abandon their coach. He was left alone on the field to face the eleven players from the opposing team. But his team cheered wildly from the bleachers: "Go get 'em, coach! We're behind you one hundred percent! You can win this game! Go, go, fight, fight, you can win the game tonight!"

Wouldn't you agree that this was a troubled football team, with a disturbing philosophy of the game?

Nevertheless, many Christians today view the body of Christ in this way. They have placed their pastor on the playing field all by himself. From the bleachers they cry: "Go get 'em, Pastor! We are behind you all the way! Win the lost! Visit the sick! Disciple the saints! Counsel the depressed! Unlock the doors early Sunday morning and lock them again after we've all gone home! And shovel the snow, too!"

This is not even close to the picture Paul paints in Ephesians 4:7-16. The laity are the ones who are called to do "the work of the ministry" (verse 12, KJV). Pastors, prophets, teachers, and evangelists are to be in the role of "equippers" (verses 11-12). From my study of Scripture along these lines, I think the best way for us to view full-time Christian workers is (continuing the sports metaphor) as a "player-coach." It is not that pastors or evangelists would never be directly involved in evangelism and discipleship. Rather, they would model these ministries in such a way that lay people can put that example into practice in their spheres of influence.

I can't believe that Paul had only "full-time" ministers in mind when he told Timothy, "And the things you have heard me say in the presence of many witnesses entrust to reliable men who will also be qualified to teach others" (2 Timothy 2:2).

We need *everybody* on the playing field! Christ calls each of us out of the bleachers and onto the turf where the real action is happening. There is an active role for every believer on God's team. Spectators and cheerleaders need not apply.

GETTING PAST THE ROADBLOCKS TO SERVANTHOOD

We know that if we want to be like Jesus, we will need to be a servant. We have looked at many passages that demonstrate the fact that we should "expect service" to be a regular part of our lives as disciples of Christ. So what is our problem? Why do so many Christians opt for cheering in the bleachers? Let me suggest a few of the roadblocks to servanthood.

1. FEAR

Let me be clear on this: It can be frightening to exercise our gifts in the body of Christ. We will make mistakes—ones that could have been avoided if we had stayed in the bleachers. We will become vulnerable—and some immature believers are all too anxious to see us blow it. Fear keeps many Christians from teaching Sunday school, doing visitation, serving in leadership, leading the choir and a host of other important ministries. Some folks won't even serve the Lord through the ministry of prayer because they are afraid that others may not approve of the words they use!

It is an incredible challenge to step out of the bleachers and onto the field. No one makes fun of the fans in the stands—snide remarks are reserved for the players, coaches and referees. We find out many things about ourselves—some good and some bad—when we commit to the cutting edge of Christian service. We need to get over our fear of failure and our fear of criticism if we are going to be useful as servants of the Lord. "For God did not give us a spirit of timidity, but a spirit of power, of love and of self-discipline" (2 Timothy 1:7).

2. SELFISHNESS

In these hectic times, many believers warm up to the excuse that they are just "too busy" to serve the Lord in the local church. Translation: "What I am doing is vastly more important than what God wants to have done." Bottom line: This person is selfish. This is why Christ talked about self-denial before He talked about following Him as a disciple: "If anyone would come after me, he must deny himself and take up his cross daily and follow me" (Luke 9:23).

It is all too easy to get caught up in our own personal problems, work schedules and family priorities. We can get tunnel vision to the extent that the only thing that matters is "me and mine." The big picture of what God wants to do in us and through us gets lost in our self-absorption. There is no denying that we all have personal problems to resolve, work schedules to keep and family priorities to maintain. But if these things are not held in balance with our need to serve and do our part in the body of Christ, we will miss the full blessing that could be ours.

3. DISTORTED VALUES

In response to a question about "who is the greatest," Jesus gave a lesson on the values of His kingdom: "If anyone wants to be first, he must be the very last, and the servant of all" (Mark 9:35).

What keeps many people from serving the Lord with their spiritual gifts is an inflated opinion of their own importance. Maybe they feel that their time, energy and financial resources are too important to be "wasted" on the church and the things of God. But this is a distorted value system. It's another illustration of this world's "upside-down" thinking. Those who would be "first" or "the greatest" in Christ's kingdom will need to excel in serving others.

Many of the people sitting in church services on any given Sunday really do feel that they are "above" any involvement with the body of Christ. They may contribute financially as a substitute for actual participation, but their attitude says, "I value my plans and my time too much to get involved with these simple folks." Unfortunately, people like this will never know the blessing, the value, the challenge and the spiritual growth that comes to those who humble themselves and find their places of service.

Fear, selfishness and distorted values can become roadblocks to service. God wants to remove these hindrances in each of our lives and set us free to serve Him with love and courage.

GETTING STARTED

Perhaps you have been persuaded that you need to get past these roadblocks and find your place of service for the Savior. Here are a few tips for getting started:

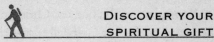

DISCOVER YOUR SPIRITUAL GIFT

As was stated in the last chapter, you are guaranteed at least one, and perhaps several, spiritual gifts as a child of God. It is important that you identify those areas of supernatural enablement. Make this a matter of urgent prayer. Talk with trusted Christian friends and spiritual leaders. Read one of the several books or booklets on spiritual gift(s) that are available at your local Christian bookstore.[1] This is a vital first step to finding your place of service.

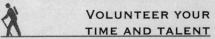

VOLUNTEER YOUR TIME AND TALENT

Some people spend years waiting around for someone to ask them to do something in the church. God will not send you a postcard stating exactly what your role in the body of Christ should be. My dad used to say, "God can't steer a parked car!" We must get moving! We may need to feel our way by trial and error, keeping an open mind for any new direction the Lord may want to take us. Take special note of those times when you felt particularly fulfilled in what you were doing.

REALIZE THAT IT
MAY NOT BE EASY

Your place in the body of Christ may not always be "easy" work. But God will ensure that it is fulfilling. Sometimes we get the impression that serving the Lord should always be "fun" or "exciting." This may not be the case at all. However, if we are plugged in where we fit and are using our spiritual gifts, we will be blessed with a deep soul satisfaction.

Expect service now that you're a Christian. The body of Christ needs your gifts and service. And you have a need to serve.

ENDNOTE

[1] Two books available from Christian Publications, Inc., are *Spiritual Gifts*, a manual for individual or group study by Bobby Clinton, and *Find and Use Your Spiritual Gifts*, by John E. Packo. Both are available from your local Christian bookstore or by calling 1-800-233-4443 or by e-mailing your order to orders@cpi-horizon.com.

CHAPTER 11

Expect Accountability

The story is told of a pastor who visited the farm of one of his parishioners. As he looked over the vast acreage of tall green cornstalks with their tassels gently swaying in the breeze against the clear blue sky, the minister exclaimed, "Well, brother, this is quite a lovely piece of land that you and the Lord have developed here!" The farmer thought for a moment, and then replied, "You should have seen this property when the Lord had it all by Himself!"

I do not think that the farmer meant to be irreverent by his comment. He was simply stating the fact that someone had to cooperate with God to turn that land into something useful. Someone had to take responsibility for cultivating and fertilizing the soil, planting and watering the seed and reaping the harvest. Without this kind of accountability, the field would have become overgrown with weeds and unsuitable for planting anything at all. Though it is true that only the Lord could ultimately make that corn grow, He used the farmer in the overall process.

The same principle applies in the arena of discipleship. Christians who are left alone with no accountability can become like neglected farmland—choked by weeds and no longer useful. Someone needs to keep plowing the hearts of new believers and planting seeds for new areas of growth. And unless the believer is willing to receive this kind of input, he will be weak and ineffective.

The Lord doesn't need our help; He could disciple new believers all by Himself, just as He could tend all the farmland in the entire world by Himself. But in His divine wisdom, He has chosen to use older Christians and the process of accountability to enable younger followers of Christ to mature in the faith. This is God's way with His children.

But just *how* can we expect accountability? To whom are we to be accountable?

ACCOUNTABILITY TO GOD

Our first line of accountability as Christians is to God Himself. Here are just a few of the many Scriptures that carry this theme:

> But I tell you that men will have to give account on the day of judgment for every careless word they have spoken. For by your

words you will be acquitted, and by your words you will be condemned. (Matthew 12:36-37)

So I strive always to keep my conscience clear before God. (Acts 24:16)

So then, each of us will give an account of himself to God. (Romans 14:12)

For no one can lay any foundation other than the one already laid, which is Jesus Christ. If any man builds on this foundation using gold, silver, costly stones, wood, hay or straw, his work will be shown for what it is, because the Day will bring it to light. It will be revealed with fire, and the fire will test the quality of each man's work. If what he has built survives, he will receive his reward. If it is burned up, he will suffer loss; he himself will be saved, but only as one escaping through the flames. (1 Corinthians 3:11-15)

Therefore judge nothing before the appointed time; wait till the Lord comes. He will bring to light what is hidden in darkness and will expose the motives of men's hearts. At that time, each will receive his praise from God. (4:5)

For we must all appear before the judgment seat of Christ, that each one may receive what is due him for the things done while in the body, whether good or bad. (2 Corinthians 5:10)

Nothing in all creation is hidden from God's sight. Everything is uncovered and laid bare before the eyes of him to whom we must give account. (Hebrews 4:13)

But they will have to give account to him who is ready to judge the living and the dead. (1 Peter 4:5)

These passages demonstrate that we need to think of our accountability both in terms of here and hereafter. We are responsible for our actions right now in our day-to-day existence. Though God is not standing over us in His physical presence waiting to blow a whistle when we commit a sin, His presence is real nonetheless. It is inescapable and unavoidable. There is simply nowhere to hide from the omnipresent One. (See Psalm 139:7-12.)

And we will ultimately answer for the "big picture" of our lives when we stand before the Lord at the final judgment. This day of reckoning is coming with the same certainty as tomorrow's sunrise. There will be no excused absences. All secrets will be revealed. Everything hidden will be exposed. This will be quite a day!

All of this may sound overwhelming and frightening, but the good news is this: we will not have to stand alone before the Judge of all the universe. As Christians, we will have our Defense Attorney with us: Christ Jesus Himself. He will represent our case to His Father. As we confess our iniquity, the Savior forgives. At that moment, He becomes our "advocate":

> If anybody does sin, we have one who speaks to the Father in our defense—Jesus Christ, the Righteous One. He is the atoning sacrifice for our sins, and not only for ours but also for the sins of the whole world" (1 John 2:1-2).

What about the sins that I don't confess before I die or before the Lord comes again? I have been asked that question many times and I'm not sure I have the complete answer. But two things can be stated with certainty.

First, the judgment seat of Christ for all believers is not about whether we will gain entrance to heaven or not—that was settled when we first believed. This day of reckoning has to do with "rewards" for our faithfulness to the Savior.

Second, we should keep current accounts with God on a daily basis. When the Lord shows us sin of any kind, we should be quick to confess it and forsake it. This kind of accountability ensures that those transgressions are canceled forever. The sin for which

WHAT TO EXPECT NOW THAT YOU BELIEVE

we have already repented will never be brought back to haunt us in this life or in the judgment to come.

I have heard people talk about the judgment day in terms of a "video" being shown of all our secret thoughts and actions so that everyone can see what we were "really" like. Of course, God will be much more creative than that! But even if such a "video" exists, our Defense Attorney, Jesus Christ, will have "edited" the final product to coincide with our confessions. Those sins have been permanently expunged from the record. In God's mind, those iniquities simply do not exist. "I, even I, am he who blots out your transgressions, for my own sake,/ and remembers your sins no more" (Isaiah 43:25). "If you, O LORD, kept a record of sins,/ O Lord, who could stand?/ But with you there is forgiveness;/ therefore you are feared" (Psalm 130:3-4).

This is why we do not need to be terrified when we ponder our accountability to God. As we walk in the light, the blood of Jesus will keep on purifying us from all sin (1 John 1:7, author's paraphrase). The New Testament goes so far as to say that we can have confidence as we stand before the Lord!

In him [Jesus] and through faith in him we may approach God with freedom and confidence. (Ephesians 3:12)

In this way, love is made complete among us so that we will have confidence on the

day of judgment, because in this world we
are like him. There is no fear in love. But
perfect love drives out fear, because fear has
to do with punishment. The one who fears is
not made perfect in love. (1 John 4:17-18)

Let me reiterate: This is not a manmade, hu-
man-based confidence in our own goodness. Our
dependence must be totally on the righteousness
of Christ. If it were not for His sacrifice on our behalf, we would never be able to enter God's holy
presence. Jesus made it all possible by taking our
sins upon Himself as if He committed each one.

Our accountability to God should be a wonderful
reminder of the grace and mercy of our dear Savior.
Rather than invoking fear and dread in our hearts,
we can celebrate the incredible forgiveness of God as
we walk in obedience to His will and His Word.

ACCOUNTABILITY TO THE BODY OF CHRIST

The second level of accountability that we can expect now that we are Christians is to the body of
Christ in a general sense. The text which was used
earlier in this chapter from Acts 24:16 goes on to include the church: "So I strive always to keep my conscience clear before God *and man*" (emphasis added.)

Jesus addressed this same issue in the context of
good churchgoing folks:

Therefore, if you are offering your gift at the altar and there remember that your brother has something against you, leave your gift there in front of the altar. First go and be reconciled to your brother; then come and offer your gift" (Matthew 5:23-24).

Many believers would like to keep their Christianity between themselves and God. If they could, they would be "holy hermits living in the hills." And let's face it—in many ways, it would be a whole lot easier to live the Christian life if we didn't have to contend with ornery folks in God's family. As pastors sometimes say with a slight smile, "I would love the ministry if it weren't for the people!"

From time to time, I hear about believers who have stopped going to church. They still love God and want to worship Him. But they got hurt by other Christians and now they find it difficult to grow spiritually in a body of believers, because they associate the church with conflict. Though this may be understandable, it is also unacceptable.

God has chosen to use both the good and the bad elements of body life in Christ to bring us to greater maturity. Though the church is far from perfect, it is the Lord's instrument to teach believers and reach unbelievers. I said earlier that the church needs you and me to serve the Lord with our gifts. But we should also know that we need the church.

The book of Acts provides several illustrations of this important dynamic of the accountability of every believer to the body of Christ.

> They devoted themselves to the apostles' teaching and to the fellowship, to the breaking of bread and to prayer. . . . All the believers were together and had everything in common. . . .
>
> All the believers were one in heart and mind. No one claimed that any of his possessions was his own, but they shared everything they had. . . .
>
> While they were worshiping the Lord and fasting, the Holy Spirit said, "Set apart for me Barnabas and Saul for the work to which I have called them." So after they had fasted and prayed, they placed their hands on them and sent them off. (2:42, 44; 4:32; 13:2-3)

In Acts 11, Peter is asked to explain his actions with regard to his ministry among the Gentiles. In Acts 15, the Council at Jerusalem was convened to discuss the teaching that had been circulated by some brothers from Judea: "Unless you are circumcised, according to the custom taught by Moses, you cannot be saved" (15:1).

The point of all of these passages is that the members of the body of Christ were accountable to the church for their ministry, their behavior and their doctrine. No one dared to assume the role of the "Lone Ranger." They understood that God had ordained a "check and balance" system in the fellowship of the saints. No man was an island. They needed each other even as we need each other today.

In Matthew 18, Christ outlines this important principle of accountability when it comes to sin in the church.

> If your brother sins against you, go and show him his fault, just between the two of you. If he listens to you, you have won your brother over. But if he will not listen, take one or two others along, so that "every matter may be established by the testimony of two or three witnesses." If he refuses to listen to them, tell it to the church; and if he refuses to listen even to the church, treat him as you would a pagan or a tax collector. (Matthew 18:15-17)

My father had to discipline a wealthy man in one of the churches he pastored. This individual had left his wife for another woman and was living in open adultery with her even though he was a member of the church. My father went to him privately and pleaded with him to return to his wife. The man refused. Next, a small group of elders joined my dad in confronting him with his sin. He still would not repent.

I will never forget that Sunday morning service when this man's membership was publicly revoked as he sat listening in the balcony. Rev. Bill Allen was simply following the prescribed method of accountability outlined by Jesus Christ. On that Sunday, the pastor had to "tell it to the church." Though this was not a pleasant experience for anyone involved, it was the right thing to do. As members of the body of Christ, we are answerable to the church for our behavior.

On another occasion, a young pastor who had been discipled by my father got away from sound doctrine. Some very unbalanced individuals convinced this young man that he had "the gift of the apostle." He began to believe that his words carried the same weight as that of any New Testament writer. He became very dogmatic about this. My father and the district superintendent met with him on several occasions, but the pastor simply would not change his mind. He had to be publicly removed from his ministry.

Thankfully, this man came to his senses several months later and was reinstated to a pastoral ministry in another state. He finally realized that as a member of the body of Christ, he was accountable to the church for his doctrine. So am I. So are you.

ACCOUNTABILITY TO SMALL GROUPS AND/OR INDIVIDUALS

There is one more level of accountability that we can expect as believers. This has to do with our need to have a small group or an individual with whom we can be totally transparent. The scriptural principle can be found in these passages:

> A friend loves at all times,
>   and a brother is born for adversity.
> (Proverbs 17:17)

> As iron sharpens iron,
>   so one man sharpens another.
> (27:17)

> Two are better than one,
>   because they have a good return for their
>   work:
> If one falls down,
>   his friend can help him up.
> But pity the man who falls
>   and has no one to help him up.
> (Ecclesiastes 4:9-10)

These three beautiful passages have a common thread which weaves its way through each verse: We need to be accountable to one trusted brother or sister, or to a small group with whom we can share confidentially. This goes beyond the general principle of being answerable to the body of Christ. In that group or with that individual we discover a special place where we can experience healing in our adversity. We can allow our iron to become sharpened. We can be lifted up when we have fallen. The loneliness of the person who does not have this kind of confidant is expressed with great emotion in Ecclesiastes 4:10: "But pity the man who falls and has no one to help him up."

Finding such a prayer partner or small group where we can freely share our struggles, temptations, failures and victories is not always an easy task. We need to be sure that this individual or prayer group can be trusted with the sometimes painful truth we may share. Nothing will push a Christian into a shell more rapidly than a betrayed confidence. This is a very serious issue and we must choose our confidants carefully, through much prayer.

I recommend that believers confide in members of the same sex. Men can relate to other men's struggles in the same way that women are more able to understand another woman's heartcry. Sharing intimate temptations and defeats with a member of the opposite sex (other than one's spouse, of course!) can lead to morally compromising scenarios. Stories of sexual involvement in the context of a counseling ministry are legion and should be a warning to us. We are simply not equipped to share these kinds of details with the opposite sex without facing strong temptations and detrimental consequences.

Are there some things that we should *never* share with any individual or small group? Probably. We must be discerning along these lines. Jesus is the ultimate "prayer partner" and "a friend who sticks closer than a brother" (Proverbs 18:24). There may be issues in your life and mine that should be brought to His attention only. But as a general rule, we need to find that individual or small group in which we feel free to "tell it like it is."

Have you found that special friend or prayer group? If you have, count yourself blessed indeed! If you have not, let me encourage you to make this a matter of urgent prayer. Be patient. Allow God to bring the person(s) of His choosing into your life according to His plan and timetable.

Now that you believe, expect accountability. Expect it in your relationship with God on a daily basis and ultimately before His throne. Count on being answerable to the body of Christ for your behavior and doctrine. And find that individual or small group with whom you can be open and honest.

Through it all, remember that accountability is a good thing. It will keep us on the cutting edge of growth in our daily walk with the Lord.

CHAPTER 12

Expect
Victory

A.B. Simpson told the story of a millionaire who found a beautiful lot on which he planned to build a mansion. The man who owned the property lived in a small, rundown cabin on the land. A generous offer was made, and the owner prepared to move. But as the seller contemplated the wealth and prestige of the buyer, he began to think about the importance of making some improvements to the existing building.

So he began to paint and patch. He called around for estimates on a new roof and new siding for the cabin. One day the millionaire decided to visit his new property. He was quite surprised to find the owner working so feverishly to spruce things up. He called him over and said, "Hey, I appreciate the fact that you are trying to fix this place

181

up for me. But don't waste your money! What I really wanted was this splendid location. When this land becomes my possession, I will tear down the old cabin and build a home of my very own."

In his book, *Wholly Sanctified*, Dr. Simpson explains how this illustrates God's desire for His children:

> This is exactly what God wants of us and waits to do in us. Each of us has a splendid site for a heavenly temple. It looks out upon eternity and commands a view of all that is glorious in the possibilities of existence, but the house that is built upon it now is a worthless wreck—it is past improving. Our patching and repairing is worse than waste. What God wants of us is simply that we give Him the possibilities of our lives and let Him build upon them a temple of holiness which He will make His own abode and which He will let us dwell in with Him as His happy guests in the house of the Lord forever.

> From the very foundations, the work must be all new and divine. He is the Author and Finisher of our faith, and the true attitude of the consecrated heart is that of a constant yielding and constant receiving.[1]

We can expect victory in the Christian life because of the great truths contained in this little parable. Consider them with me now.

RECOGNIZE OUR INADEQUACY

The landowner was made to realize the inadequacy of his dilapidated cabin to meet the high expectations of the millionaire. In the same way, we must recognize our own inadequacy to please God and live a victorious Christian life through our own strength and virtue. Paul confronted this reality in his own life in Romans 7:

> We know that the law is spiritual; but I am unspiritual, sold as a slave to sin. I do not understand what I do. For what I want to do I do not do, but what I hate I do. And if I do what I do not want to do, I agree that the law is good. As it is, it is no longer I myself who do it, but it is sin living in me. I know that nothing good lives in me, that is, in my sinful nature. For I have the desire to do what is good, but I cannot carry it out. For what I do is not the good I want to do; no, the evil I do not want to do—this I keep on doing. . . .
>
> So I find this law at work: When I want to do good, evil is right there with me. For in my inner being, I delight in God's law; but I see another law at work in the members of my

body, waging war against the law of my mind and making me a prisoner of the law of sin at work within my members. What a wretched man I am! Who will rescue me from this body of death? (Romans 7:14-19; 21-24)

The phrase "body of death" is an allusion to a particularly gruesome Roman torture. Some prisoners who were sentenced to die were tied arm-to-arm and leg-to-leg with a dead corpse. They would walk the streets crying out for help: "Please, somebody release me from this corpse! I beg you, please cut me loose!" Of course, anyone caught assisting a prisoner in this fashion would face his own execution. Eventually, the poison from this dead, rotting body would slowly kill the prisoner.

The apostle Paul carefully chose this illustration to highlight the intense warfare that is going on between the old nature and the new nature. The carnal nature has an opposing agenda to that of the Christ nature. "The mind of sinful man is death, but the mind controlled by the Spirit is life and peace; the sinful mind is hostile to God. It does not submit to God's law, nor can it do so. Those controlled by the sinful nature cannot please God" (8:6-8).

This realization of our inability to live the Christian life occurs at different points for each of us. Some believers discover this almost simultaneously with their salvation experience. Most of us tend to come to this conclusion a bit later in our walk with God after we have faced some trials, temptations, persecutions and doubts. But in His time, it dawns on us just as it was revealed to Paul: We are not adequate in ourselves to practice Christianity in a manner that truly glorifies God. We may want to please Him and we may put forth genuine, earnest efforts, but we find ourselves powerless to do so.

The inadequacy of the old nature may be revealed through such things as a stubborn sinful habit that cannot be broken, tense relationships at home or in the workplace, a hot temper, lustful thoughts and behaviors, spiritual apathy or selfishness. Any or all of these may point to our need for a deeper work of God's Spirit.

In this sense, Romans 7 is the story of all of us. When we are first saved, we are "on fire for the Lord." We are driven to gladden the heart of God. We seem to have unlimited energy to work for the Savior. Anxious to study the Bible and spend time in prayer, we grow by leaps and bounds during those early weeks and months. Then some kind of failure becomes apparent. We begin to notice that we simply cannot live up to our ideals as a Christian. We resolve to do better only to become aware of the fact that we are caught in a vicious cycle.

The question Paul asks in Romans 7:24—"Who will rescue me from this body of death?"—he answers in the very next verse: "Thanks be to God—through Jesus Christ our Lord!" Let's see how this can happen.

RECKONING OUR DEATH AND RESURRECTION

Christ rescues us from the ravages of the old nature through a process that Paul refers to as "reckoning":

> If we have been united with him like this in his death, we will certainly also be united with him in his resurrection. For we know that our old self was crucified with him so that the body of sin might be done away with, that we should no longer be slaves to sin—because anyone who has died has been freed from sin.
>
> Now if we died with Christ, we believe that we will also live with him. For we know that since Christ was raised from the dead, he cannot die again; death no longer has mastery over him. The death he died, he died to sin once for all; but the life he lives, he lives to God.
>
> In the same way, count ["reckon," KJV] yourselves dead to sin but alive to God in Christ Jesus. (6:5-11)

The word "count" or "reckon" simply means "agree." We are to agree with God that when Jesus died on the cross, our old nature died with Him. When He rose from the dead three days later in power over death and sin, we, too, were resurrected with power over death and sin.

We must move this truth from the category of "factual" to that of "actual" in our experience. It is a fact that our carnal nature lost its power over us because of the death and resurrection of the Savior. But that only becomes actual in your life and mine when we agree with God—when we "reckon" it to be true right here and right now. We are both "dead" and "alive" at the same time—dead to the old nature, alive to the new nature.

In Romans 12:1, Paul urges us to offer our bodies as "living sacrifices." This may sound like an oxymoron, since a sacrifice is something that has been killed and burned on an altar—quite dead, we would presume. How can something that is "living" be referred to as a "sacrifice"? This passage could be called God's "Wanted" poster:

> WANTED:
> Christians—
> Dead *and* Alive!

How does it look to be both "dead" and "alive" at the same time? I want to illustrate this by showing ten contrasting characteristics of the carnal nature versus the Christ nature. As we consider both sides of this ledger, we begin to realize the glorious exchange that can take place when we reckon ourselves dead to sin and alive to God. By agreeing with God about what took place at the cross and through the resurrection, we can expect victory to be ours.

CARNAL NATURE	CHRIST NATURE
1. Gossip	Encouragement
2. Oversensitivity	Sensitivity to others
3. Temper tantrums	Anger for sin
4. Lust	Love
5. Bitterness	Forgiveness
6. Divisive	Reconciling
7. Doubt	Faith
8. Demanding my rights	Denying my rights
9. Selfishness	Selflessness
10. Apathy for God	Apathy for the world

1. GOSSIP VS. ENCOURAGEMENT

The carnal nature loves to gossip: "He did? She did? No! Give me the details. Really? I can't believe it!" Why do we love to talk behind someone else's back? The answer is simple: We can put someone else down while lifting ourselves up. The implication is, "Well, you and I wouldn't do this, but did you hear about so-and-so?"

Inevitably, gossip always gets exaggerated and expanded. Perhaps you heard about the one snoop who said to the other, "Tell me more!" The other snoop replied, "I can't tell you more—I've already told you more than I heard!" Funny and true.

What a contrast we discover in the Christ nature. When we are controlled by His Spirit, we will seek to encourage people in every way. We will have a passion to build up rather than tear down. When we reckon that old nature dead and exchange it for the new nature, we will be looking for ways to edify others. This is such an important ministry. So many need an uplifting word in a world that can wear us down with criticism.

 ## 2. OVERSENSITIVITY VS. SENSITIVITY TO OTHERS

So many Christians seem to go through life with a chip on their shoulders. One has to be extremely careful in approaching such a person; no one knows what might set them off. These people are always getting their feelings hurt by others. Life for them becomes a kind of "woe is me" existence. Because the carnal nature always "looks out for number one," these folks are often oblivious to the needs of others.

Contrast this with the wonderful nature of Jesus Christ. His nature is characterized by a genuine sensitivity to others. The Christ-life is so very different from the self-life. When He lives His life in us, our eyes are opened to those around us who have been hurt along life's way. Rather than focusing on our own troubles and concerns, we "carry each other's burdens, and in this way . . . fulfill the law of Christ" (Galatians 6:2).

3. TEMPER TANTRUMS VS. ANGER FOR SIN

A personal testimony fits well here. As the youngest of five boys, I had quite a temper during my childhood and teen years. In a very competitive environment, I was a poor loser. I can remember breaking Ping-Pong™ paddles when I lost a game. When I got to college, God began to do a work in my life. During a conference on Spirit-filled living, I responded to the invitation and asked the Lord to take control of my life. On the top of my list was my wild and erratic temper.

Shortly after I had asked the Lord to fill me with His Holy Spirit, I had an experience that confirmed His powerful work. I was working out with weights. (I have hard muscles—they are hard to find!) As I was adjusting the barbell, one of my fingers got mashed between the weights. Out of my mouth came a sudden and unexpected phrase: "Praise the Lord!"

I was stunned. Under "normal" conditions, the old Tom Allen would have thrown that barbell through the window in anger and disgust! (Some people might have expected me to burst out with a volley of foul language, but swearing had never been a problem for me. My mother took care of that with Ivory Soap when I was just a little boy.)

But the new Tom Allen reacted quite differently by saying, "Praise the Lord!" I walked over to the mirror and asked myself, "So—who said that?" It was as if Jesus spoke audibly to me back through that mirror: "I said it, Tom. It's Christ in you, the hope of glory."

The Lord does not want to "help" us with our temper tantrums. Jesus is not interested in merely "reducing" our level of rage. He wants us to agree with Him that the old nature from which our anger arises is dead. That carnal nature no longer has power to control our behavior. We have been set free by Christ's resurrection to be men, women and young people who are controlled by the Holy Spirit.

There is a place for anger. "In your anger, do not sin. Do not let the sun go down while you are still angry" (Ephesians 4:26). A friend of mine preached a sermon on this text entitled, "How to Be Good and Mad." There is a place for righteous indignation. We should be angry about sin in our own lives and wickedness in our society. We are not, however, permitted to become angry because someone mistreated or misrepresented us. We should not lose our temper because we lost a game. Christ can become our victory over this kind of anger.

4. Lust vs. Love

Another characteristic of the carnal nature is lust. I would define this as any inordinate passion for something that will eventually harm us. There is nothing wrong with the natural desire for sex or food. In the right context and in proper quantities, these things can be beneficial and bring glory to God. But the Adamic nature always wants to push beyond the normal boundaries of holiness. In our carnal frame of mind, we have strong desires for sexual relationships outside the bonds of marriage. We would choose too much food, and food that is not good for us.

Whereas lust seeks its own pleasure, genuine, biblical love seeks someone else's highest good. This is the essence of the Christ nature. Instead of looking for ways to satisfy ourselves, we will be on a mission to please God and others. Interestingly enough, when that is our quest, we find the real satisfaction we were searching for all along.

5. Bitterness vs. Forgiveness

The self-life wants to hold on tenaciously to those painful memories from the past. Unforgiveness is at first a sweet morsel to be savored. It is a way to get even with those who have offended us in some fashion. I have spoken with young women on Christian college campuses who were raped or molested by trusted spiritual leaders in their home church. Many of them have said to me, "Mr. Allen, I just can't forgive them." If they mean they can't do it without God's help, I absolutely agree. There is no way that any of us could pardon others in our own strength.

But in Christ Jesus, there is hope to become a forgiving person. It literally becomes a matter of the Lord Jesus acquitting that offending individual through us. This is another aspect of Colossians 1:27, "Christ in you, the hope of glory." Christ in you and me is the only hope of being able to forgive those who have sinned against us.

6. DIVISIVE VS. RECONCILING

Do you know people who are always stirring up trouble? They seem to thrive on division. Many things could be said about such persons, but one thing is certain: They are not filled with the Holy Spirit. They are being dominated by the carnal nature. In fact, this "divisive spirit" is on a long list of the "acts of the sinful nature" along with things like sexual immorality, idolatry, witchcraft, drunkenness and orgies (Galatians 5:19-21).

The Christ nature is marked by its passion for reconciliation:

193

Therefore, if anyone is in Christ, he is a new creation; the old has gone, the new has come! All this is from God, who reconciled us to himself through Christ . . . not counting men's sins against them. And he has committed to us the message of reconciliation. (2 Corinthians 5:17-19)

Believers who are filled with God's Spirit have a natural desire to get involved in the ministry of reconciliation. Rather than trying to start a fight, they will try to stop it. Instead of dividing the body of Christ, they will seek to unify that body. This is the Christ-life for your life and mine.

7. DOUBT VS. FAITH

We can also exchange our old nature's tendency to doubt for the new nature's ascendancy to faith. We allow Christ to reproduce His faith in us by reckoning that carnal nature, with all of its disbelief, to no longer have control in our lives. This will make a huge difference in our prayer life, and in our ministry to others who are struggling.

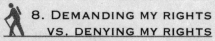

8. DEMANDING MY RIGHTS VS. DENYING MY RIGHTS

I've heard disgruntled believers at a church board meeting say, "Well, I've got my rights, you know!" My reply is usually this: "I'm certainly glad that Jesus didn't have His rights. He could have called 10,000 angels to destroy the world and set Him free. That was His 'right'. But He chose to give that all up to die for us."

The Christ nature teaches us that the only right we really have is to give all of our rights back to God. This is part of what Jesus meant when He said that anyone who wants to be His disciple must "deny himself and take up his cross daily" (Luke 9:23). We must voluntarily give up our supposed "rights" in order to be able to follow our Lord without any preconditions.

9. SELFISHNESS VS. SELFLESSNESS

Here again we see the stark contrast between the carnal nature and the Christ nature, between spiritual victory and spiritual defeat. One nature wants to take. The other wants to give. One looks out for number one. The other looks out for everyone. We can agree with God about the fact that the old nature of selfishness will no longer be our master. We can choose to be slaves to the new nature.

10. APATHY FOR GOD VS. APATHY FOR THE WORLD

Many Christians wonder what happens to their eagerness and enthusiasm for the things of God after they have been believers for a few years. Apathy sets in. They just don't seem to care like they once did.

One reason for this is rooted in the carnal nature. Remember, "the sinful mind is hostile to God. It does not submit to God's law, nor can it do so" (Romans 8:7). The flesh will get us all enthused about the things of the flesh.

In the opposite way, the Holy Spirit will get us excited about the things of the Spirit. When we are under His control, we will be interested in and moved by the issues relating to God and His Word. Spiritual things will turn our crank.

Consider this list of ten contrasting characteristics and note that we are not merely trying to achieve a "passing grade" by getting 7 or 8 out of 10. The Holy Spirit of God wants to exchange *everything* on the right side for *everything* on the left side! And He can do this as we "reckon" or "agree" with God about the implications of the death and resurrection of Jesus Christ.

How does it look to be dead to the flesh and alive to Christ? A minister friend of mine used a funeral scenario to demonstrate how this would look. Pretend that someone you know has just died. We'll call him Jim. Envision Jim laying in the casket as mourners pass by. Suddenly, something very strange happens. Two of the guests walk up to the casket and start to gossip: "Did you know that Jim . . . ?" Vicious backbiting ensues. Now what's Jim going to do? Will he sit up in his casket and defend himself against this malicious slander? Of course not! He's dead! You can say anything you want behind his back, and he won't retaliate.

During this odd funeral another person walks up to the casket. In an emotional outburst, she yells: "I've always wanted to say this to you, Jim . . . " And she proceeds with some very unkind words for the deceased. Will Jim tell her to shut up? I don't think so. You see, he's dead. Speak freely to Jim. He won't respond angrily—he won't respond at all.

Next, we see a mischievous man heading for Jim's casket. Looking around to be sure no one catches him, he punches Jim in the face right there in the casket! (Aren't you glad this is not a true story?!) Would Jim sit up quickly to find the man who did this? Would he cry out, "I will get even with you!"? No. Jim's dead. Punch him. Pinch him. Kick him. He will not be getting even with his attacker.

As crude as this illustration is, it drives home a powerful point. When we are dead to self and alive to Christ, people can gossip about us and we won't have to find out who said what to whom. Folks can say mean, cruel things right to our face and we won't need to snap back at them. Someone may even harm us physically and we would not retaliate. How are these things possible? Paul said it best: "I have been crucified with Christ and I no longer live, but Christ lives in me. The life I live in the body, I live by faith in the Son of God, who loved me and gave himself for me" (Galatians 2:20).

REDEDICATING OUR LIVES DAILY

The "reckoning" described above is usually a "crisis" experience in the life of the believer. When we come to that place of full surrender to God, admitting that we cannot successfully live the Christian life through our own strength, it is often a very emotional encounter with the Holy Spirit. As wonderful as this may be, such a crisis must be followed by a process.

Someone has wisely said, "The problem with a living sacrifice is that it keeps crawling off the altar." Or, as one man so profoundly expressed it, "I thought I was dead to the flesh. I found out I was just in a coma!"

One problem is that the very terms we use can be misleading. To be "dead to the flesh," for example, does not mean "the flesh is dead"! The phrase in Romans 6:6, "that the body of sin might be done away with," would be more accurately translated "that the body of sin might be rendered inoperative."

This is why Paul insists that we must "keep on counting" ourselves dead to sin. The verb tense is present continuous for a very important reason: The carnal nature will regularly attempt to regain control. The apostle goes on: "Therefore do not let sin reign in your mortal body so that you obey its evil desires. . . . For sin shall not be your master, because you are not under law, but under grace" (Romans 6:12, 14).

The sin nature will never be "dead" in the sense of eradication while we dwell here in these mortal bodies. Sin's penalty has been paid and its power has been overthrown in our lives. Someday (see the next chapter) we will be completely free from the very presence of sin. But even though sin is present with us now, it does not have to be president! One of my professors used to say, "Spirit-filled Christians are not *sinless*, but by God's grace, they will *sin less*!" We're not perfect yet, but we are moving in the direction of perfection.

What should we do if we succumb to the flesh in a particular area and fall into sin? We must quickly repent and get right back on the highway to holiness! Some believers mistakenly assume that being filled with the Spirit means that they have "arrived." Actually, this is commencement, not arrival. We will be even more sensitive to sin and more willing to humble ourselves as God deals with us because His Spirit has full sway in our hearts. (Review the end of Chapter 8.)

Expect victory! Jesus provided everything we need to live a victorious Christian life on a daily basis. He paved the way for our triumph. "But thanks be to God, who always leads us in triumphal procession in Christ" (2 Corinthians 2:14).

ENDNOTE

[1] A.B. Simpson, *Wholly Sanctified* (Camp Hill, PA: Christian Publications, Inc., 1991), pp. 16-17.

CHAPTER 13

*Expect
Eternal Life*

My father died on March 1, 1992. It was sudden, but not unexpected; he had been struggling with heart disease for several years. My mother passed away on Mother's Day in 1994 after a five-year battle with Hepatitis C. We were never able to pinpoint where she contracted this deadly disease. I was extremely close to both of my parents, and I miss them very much.

One day during the writing of this manuscript, my youngest daughter, Amanda, was playing a song on the piano that my mother loved. I burst into tears at the thought that Mom could not be here to listen to this very accomplished young musician. Both Mom and Dad will miss the teen years, the college years and so many other things that are ahead for both of my daughters. This is one of the many "downsides" of the death of a human being. But this much I know: Both my parents expected eternal life.

Life beyond the grave is a concept that often seems distant and removed to us. But when a close friend or loved one dies, our interest can be suddenly and dramatically stirred. Death is a traumatic event in every way. Mourning is appropriate because we will not see that person again in this world. Loneliness, pain and despair are normal feelings that should not be suppressed. We must find appropriate ways to express our grief.

During and after the funeral, we must deal with the reality of Ecclesiastes 3:11: "He has made everything beautiful in its time. He has also set eternity in the hearts of men; yet they cannot fathom what God has done from beginning to end."

When Bill and Madonna Allen died, our family did not "grieve like the rest of men, who have no hope" (1 Thessalonians 4:13). They expected eternal life because Jesus promised it and provided for it:

> But Christ has indeed been raised from the dead, the firstfruits of those who have fallen asleep. For since death came through a man, the resurrection of the dead comes also through a man. For as in Adam all die, so in Christ all will be made alive" (1 Corinthians 15:20-22).

I have quite often pondered the present state of my parents. What must it be like in paradise? Are they aware of things down here on earth? If so, to what extent? Have they met their friends and relatives who preceded them in death? If they had the choice to return to this earth, would they want to? Or does this world pale in comparison to what they are now experiencing? I don't have the answers to all of these questions. But let's explore what we do know.

EXPECT ETERNAL LIFE NOW

When we repent of our sins and trust Christ to be our Savior, we become the recipients of eternal life at that moment. Jesus stated this clearly in John's Gospel:

> Just as Moses lifted up the snake in the desert, so the Son of Man must be lifted up, that everyone who believes in him may have eternal life.
>
> For God so loved the world that he gave his one and only Son, that whoever believes in him shall not perish but have eternal life. . . .
>
> Whoever believes in the Son has eternal life, but whoever rejects the Son will not see life, for God's wrath remains on him. . . .
> My sheep listen to my voice; I know them, and they follow me. I give them eternal life,

and they shall never perish; no one can snatch them out of my hand. (John 3:14-16, 36; 10:27-28)

The Savior was talking about eternal life as a present possession for those who "believe in the Son." He did not imply that everlasting life began at the moment of physical death. When we are born again, we will never die spiritually. The opposite is true for those who reject Christ. The process of eternal death has already begun. Only one thing can reverse that unenviable plunge into separation from God—the humble prayer of repentance and faith.

SLEEPING SAINTS

In First Thessalonians 4, Paul outlines the blessed hope of eternal life for every born-again child of God:

> Brothers, we do not want you to be ignorant about those who fall asleep, or to grieve like the rest of men, who have no hope. We believe that Jesus died and rose again and so we believe that God will bring with Jesus those who have fallen asleep in him. According to the Lord's own word, we tell you that we who are still alive, who are left till the coming of the Lord, will certainly not precede those who have fallen asleep. For the Lord himself will come down from heaven, with a

loud command, with the voice of the archangel and with the trumpet call of God, and the dead in Christ will rise first. After that, we who are still alive and are left will be caught up together with them in the clouds to meet the Lord in the air. And so we will be with the Lord forever. Therefore encourage each other with these words. (4:13-18)

Christians who have died are in a state of rest in the conscious presence of Jesus. The Savior told the thief on the cross, "Today you will be with me in paradise" (Luke 23:43). Triumphant tranquillity and perfect peace are waiting for the moment when the Lord Jesus Christ Himself comes down from heaven "with a loud command, with the voice of the archangel and with the trumpet call of God" (1 Thessalonians 4:16). This is the glorious existence of those who have already died in the Lord.

THE LAST SHALL BE FIRST

There is a specific order of events surrounding the second coming of Christ. The very first ones to receive their new bodies will be the "sleeping saints"—those believers who died before His return. "We who are still alive, who are left till the coming of the Lord, will certainly not precede those who have fallen asleep. . . . the dead in Christ will rise first." (4:15, 16).

I think this is a good example of the scriptural principle concerning the values of Christ's kingdom: "But many who are first will be last, and many who are last will be first" (Matthew 19:30).

My parents and grandparents will beat me to those new bodies. Most of us can think of several loved ones who will put on the imperishable before we will. What an exciting moment! In an instant, everything will change:

> Listen, I tell you a mystery: We will not all sleep, but we will all be changed—in a flash, in the twinkling of an eye, at the last trumpet. For the trumpet will sound, the dead will be raised imperishable, and we will be changed. For the perishable must clothe itself with the imperishable, and the mortal with immortality. . . .
> "Where, O death, is your victory?
> Where, O death, is your sting?"
> (1 Corinthians 15:51-53, 55)

This is the moment when we will be liberated from the very presence of sin. "But we know that when he appears, we shall be like him, for we shall see him as he is" (1 John 3:2). What a transformation! We will have new bodies that do not even have the potential for evil. The immensity of this change is beyond the description of any language.

CAUGHT UP TOGETHER IN THE CLOUDS

Most of us have flown in airplanes. We remember the mystery of climbing up into the clouds. Then suddenly, that darkened fuselage flames with sunlight as we break through that last layer of clouds. Our meeting with Christ will be something like this, but it would be impossible to describe it. Paul gave it a try: "After that, we who are still alive and are left will be caught up together with them in the clouds to meet the Lord in the air" (1 Thessalonians 4:17).

We've all had important meetings in our lifetime, but this one will be the most important and blessed of all! We won't even need a jet plane. Energized by the resurrection power of God Almighty, we will be catapulted into the sky for the greatest gathering we have ever experienced. Carrie Breck tried to capture this moment in the famous hymn, "Face to Face":

Face to face with Christ, my Saviour,
Face to face what will it be— —
When with rapture I behold Him,
Jesus Christ, who died for me!
Face to face shall I behold Him,
Far beyond the starry sky;
Face to face in all His glory,
I shall see Him by and by![1]

There is a double blessing alluded to here in First Thessalonians 4:17. Paul tells us that we will be "caught up together." Who is he talking about? Those who have died will be reunited with those who are alive when Jesus returns. It's a grand reunion with our friends and loved ones followed by our first face-to-face meeting with our lovely Savior.

It just doesn't get any better than this! Not only will we be with the Lover of our soul, but as an added benefit we will be privileged to celebrate the entire event with long-lost loved ones. Try to picture this; feel this; contemplate the joy of this coming event.

WITH THE LORD FOREVER

As much as I enjoy family reunions, there is one thing I always hate: They have to end. Eventually, everyone has to pack up and return to their homes across the country. But Paul describes a reunion for the family of God that will never end! "And so we will be with the Lord forever" (4:17).

Listen to John's description of the wonder, beauty and majesty of eternal life:

> Then I saw a new heaven and a new earth, for the first heaven and the first earth had passed away, and there was no longer any sea. I saw the Holy City, the new Jerusalem, coming down out of heaven from God, prepared as a bride beautifully dressed for her husband.

And I heard a loud voice from the throne saying, "Now the dwelling of God is with men, and he will live with them. They will be his people, and God himself will be with them and be their God. He will wipe every tear from their eyes. There will be no more death or mourning or crying or pain, for the old order of things has passed away." . . .

Then the angel showed me the river of the water of life, as clear as crystal, flowing from the throne of God and of the Lamb down the middle of the great street of the city. On each side of the river stood the tree of life, bearing twelve crops of fruit, yielding its fruit every month. And the leaves of the tree are for the healing of the nations. No longer will there be any curse. The throne of God and of the Lamb will be in the city, and his servants will serve him. They will see his face, and his name will be on their foreheads. There will be no more night. They will not need the light of a lamp or the light of the sun, for the Lord God will give them light. And they will reign for ever and ever. (Revelation 21:1-4; 22:1-5)

When my father preached through the book of Revelation, he pointed out that phrase in Revelation 21:1—"no longer any sea." He explained that the "sea" is what separates people here on planet

Earth. I can remember how this illustration hit home for our family at that time. The firstborn, Peggy, was serving the Lord in Southeast Asia with her husband, Bob and their children. There was a lot of ocean between us! In an attempt to describe the glory of eternal bliss, the apostle John employed this powerful word picture to help us realize that in heaven, nothing will ever again be able to separate us from the Triune God or our Christian friends and loved ones.

I heard a description of eternity once that was helpful to me. It is obviously limited because of the vastness of the subject matter, but instructive nonetheless. Pretend that the earth is one solid mass of firmly packed dirt. Every one million years, a tiny hummingbird flies to the surface of the earth and pecks just once at this huge dirt ball. After all the trips it would take to dismantle the entire earth one peck at a time, that would still not be even one second of eternity.

Yes, there is a reunion up ahead for every born-again believer that will never, never end! No more funerals. No more tearful good-byes. No more parting of the ways. No more announcements of "I will miss you!" We will be together with our precious Lord for all eternity. What a wonderful promise! What an incentive to be "all for Jesus" right here and right now! What a motivation to build bridges of love to unsaved friends, relatives, work associates and neighbors so that they can join God's family and celebrate with us in this grand reunion!

With deep gratitude in our hearts, dear brothers and sisters in Christ, let us expect eternal life. It is a gift that cost us nothing. But it cost our precious Savior everything.

ENDNOTE

[1] Grant Colfax Tullar, "Face to Face," *Hymns of the Christian Life* (Camp Hill, PA: Christian Publications, Inc., 1978), # 387.

What Not to Expect

The purpose of this book has been to reveal what a believer can expect in his or her Christian walk. We have learned that we can expect forgiveness, joy and peace. We can also anticipate trials, temptations, persecutions and doubts. Thank God that from these difficulties we can expect growth. We will also be privileged to expect gifts, service and accountability. And we can count on victory here and eternal life hereafter. Even the seemingly "negative" items on this list can become a plus in our relationship with the Lord.

But the title of this book implies another question: Are there some things we should not expect? Let's consider that in these closing pages.

DON'T EXPECT AN EASY ROAD

Jesus was brutally honest about the fact that we must not plan on a life of ease and comfort when we follow Him:

> Enter through the narrow gate. For wide is the gate and broad is the road that leads to destruction, and many enter through it. But small is the gate and narrow the road that leads to life, and only a few find it. (Matthew 7:13-14)

> Make every effort to enter through the narrow door, because many, I tell you, will try to enter and will not be able to. (Luke 13:24)

The word "narrow" used here refers to "anguish," "distress" or "groaning." In short, it is a difficult way. Part of the difficulty is the fact that the "broad" way looks so appealing. People going with the flow of this world have their space to spread out and do their own thing. But one artist captured the essence of Christ's teaching here. He painted the way of Christ with a narrow entrance—but the pathway became wider over the course of the believer's pilgrimage to heaven. The way of the world began with a wide gate which became more and more narrow on its way to eternal separation from God.

Paul urges us to "Endure hardship with us like a good soldier of Christ Jesus" (2 Timothy 2:3). Military imagery is scattered throughout the Bible in describing our sojourn on earth as disciples of the Lord Jesus. We are called soldiers because we are in a battle. It is not just a battle for our own soul, but also the eternal struggle for the souls of others who need Jesus. And this is a battle that will be fought to some degree every day we are alive on this planet.

Don't expect an easy way. I need to be reminded of this periodically. I find myself being "surprised" by difficulties I encounter even though I am well aware of what Peter and Paul said about this. "Do not be surprised at the painful trial you are suffering, as though something strange were happening to you" (1 Peter 4:12). "We must go through many hardships to enter the kingdom of God" (Acts 14:22).

Perhaps you are experiencing a particularly difficult week, month or year as you are reading these pages. Let me offer this word of encouragement in the words of a great old song: it will be worth it all when we see Jesus! The way will be difficult, but our Lord will never leave us or forsake us.

DON'T EXPECT EVERYONE TO LIKE YOU

Becoming a Christian does not automatically mean that everyone is going to love us and appreciate us. Some believers seem to go through life on the quest to get every person they meet to like them. Paul offered a practical word on this: "If it is possible, as far as it depends on you, live at peace with everyone" (Romans 12:18).

The clear implication of the text is that it will *not* always be possible to be at peace with everyone. We will have personality clashes with certain individuals. We won't like everyone the same and not everyone will like us. We won't see eye-to-eye with other people on doctrinal issues, styles of worship, principles for raising children and a host of other matters. We really do need to learn what it means to "agree to disagree agreeably."

This is a particularly hard pill to swallow in the church among fellow believers. It would seem logical that a group of people who all love the same Savior would love and appreciate each other equally. But this is simply not the case. You and I will be naturally drawn to some folks and repelled by others. It's an inevitable occurrence. We should not expect to be loved and appreciated by everyone.

Pastors are probably more susceptible to this false expectation than anyone else. Many ministers lose sleep trying to scheme ways to get certain parishioners to love and respect them. But it's not going to happen in every case. Think of the greatest pastor you have ever known and I can tell you at least one thing about him whether I've met him or not: He has his enemies! Some people do not like him. How do I know this? Because human nature is what it is.

DON'T EXPECT PERFECTION

The only person who has ever lived a perfect Christian life is Jesus Christ. He is the only One who has achieved that honor. This is precisely why we worship Him, rather than any other person or thing. Every other religious leader had flaws. But not Jesus. He was "tempted in every way, just as we are—yet was without sin" (Hebrews 4:15).

In Chapter 13, I discussed the joyous reality of our deliverance from the very presence of sin. This will occur when we receive our new bodies en route to our eternal home. But we cannot expect perfection while trapped in these flesh-and-blood bodies. We can and should be moving in the direction of perfection, but we are not there yet.

And just as we cannot expect perfection from ourselves, we should not hold our breath waiting to find it in anyone else. My wife was recently reminded about a statement she made to one of my sisters just prior to our wedding: "Tom is the perfect man." Well, twenty years later, we are all having a good laugh about that comment! It didn't take her long to find out how mistaken she was.

Do not look for absolute perfection in anyone but Jesus Christ. He is the only One who will never fail us, never disappoint us, never lie to us, never cheat us. We shouldn't be surprised when others fall short in these areas. Husbands and wives need to be particularly plugged into this truth. If you expect your partner to perfectly meet all your needs, prepare to become disillusioned. This is why a good marriage keeps focused on Christ, who never fails.

DON'T EXPECT TO HAVE ALL THE ANSWERS

It is true that becoming a Christian will give us added wisdom and insight. When our spiritual eyes are opened, we reach whole new levels of understanding about God, ourselves and the world around us. The assumption might be that we would become some sort of "know-it-all." This is, however, a false expectation.

We won't have the answers to every question that comes along. This is because of our limitations as mere human beings. But it is also because we have been called to a life of faith. "Without faith it is impossible to please God" (Hebrews 11:6). Our Lord wants us to trust Him even when we cannot trace Him. He wants us to believe in the darkness what He showed us in the light.

How well I remember my arrogance during the early years of college. I stayed up for hours debating roommates and other classmates about the finer points of doctrine. Back then, I thought I was just on the verge of sorting it all out. But as time has passed, my study of God's Word and my experience in life have demonstrated to me that I do not have all the answers. And I won't have them any time in the next, say, fifty years!

This can be an extremely liberating realization. Sometimes the wisest response to a question is simply, "I don't know, but I'll try to find out." Humbling? Yes. Genuine? Absolutely. And we never know how our lowliness along these lines might help someone else who struggled with the assumption that he or she had to be "The Answer Person."

Don't expect an easy road.

Don't expect everyone to like you.

Don't expect perfection.

Don't expect to have all the answers.

A PRAYER FOR YOU

I offer this prayer for each reader as a conclusion to the book:

Dear Lord,

I thank You for all those who have read these pages. I thank You that they have given their hearts to You. Help them to be realistic about both what they should and should not expect as a Christian. Give them strength in their trials, joy and comfort in their blessings and hope for eternal life. Help us all to live in the light of that great reunion of the family of God when we will worship You together around Your throne. In the strong name of Jesus I pray. Amen.

Study Guide

BY TOM ALLEN

FOR PERSONAL STUDY

Settle into your favorite chair with your Bible, a pen or pencil, a notebook and this book. Read a chapter at a time, marking portions that seem significant to you. Write in the margins, particularly noting those issues that challenge you. Look up relevant Scripture passages. Then turn to the questions listed in this study guide. You can trace your progress by recording your answers, thoughts, feelings and questions in the notebook. Refer to the text of the book and the Scriptures as you allow the questions to enlarge your thinking. And pray. Ask God to give you a discerning mind for truth and a greater love and appreciation for Himself.

FOR GROUP STUDY

If you are leading or hosting a group study, there are a number of things you can do to help make it a successful learning experience for everyone.

Plan ahead. Before meeting with the group, read and mark the chapter as if you were preparing for personal study. Glance through the questions provided, making mental notes of how you might contribute to your group's discussion. Bring a Bible along with this book to your meeting. Make sure everyone has their own copy of the book and reads at least the Introduction and Chapter 1 before the first lesson.

Offer an environment that promotes discussion. Comfortable chairs arranged in a casual circle invite people to talk, to listen, to respond to each other and to learn together. Everyone should be seated so that they can have eye contact with everyone else. If the group is larger than a half-dozen members, you may find it helpful to break into smaller discussion groups during some parts of the lesson.

Involve as many as possible. Group learning works best if everyone can participate at some point. If you are a "natural talker," pause before you enter the conversation. Then ask a quiet person what he or she thinks. If you are a "natural listener," don't hesitate to jump into the discussion. Others can only benefit from your thoughts when you express them verbally. As you lead the study, be careful not to dominate the discussion; help the group members make their own discoveries.

Pace the study. The questions for each lesson are designed to last thirty to forty-five minutes. Early questions form the framework for later discussion, so don't rush by so quickly that you miss a valuable foundation point. As you lead the study, you should keep an eye on the time and the flow of discussion, but also ask everyone in the group to assist in keeping the study moving at an even pace.

Pray for each other. Prayer should be offered during each lesson, but also make a commitment to pray for each other during the week.

COMPONENTS OF THE LESSONS

Each session includes the following features:

- *Lesson Topic:* a brief statement summarizing the lesson.
- *Fellowship Primer:* an activity or discussion issue to get acquainted with the lesson topic and/or each other.
- *Key Questions* to encourage individual or group discovery and application.
- *Prayer Focus:* suggestions for turning one's learning into prayer.
- *Assignments* to complete prior to the next lesson.

LESSON 1
EXPECT FORGIVENESS

LESSON TOPIC

The nature and extent of the forgiveness that we can expect from God when we ask Christ to become our Savior.

FELLOWSHIP PRIMER

Ask the group to share true-life "modern versions" of the New Testament story of the prodigal son from Luke 15:11-32. These stories may include one's own personal testimony or someone else's. What were the similarities to the story as Jesus told it and the way it unfolds for people today?

KEY QUESTIONS

1. What was it that Steve could not understand about his father's reaction to Jack's return?
2. What illustrations from everyday life could help us understand the concept of "forgiveness" as depicted in the Bible?
3. When did the "hug and kiss" take place according to Luke 15:20, and why is this significant?
4. Why can't we just pay the penalty for our sins by ourselves?
5. How can we "deserve" God's forgiveness?

6. Discuss the implications of the story from Chuck Colson about the prison named Humaita.
7. What are the "limitations" of God's forgiveness?
8. What would be our most important response to others based on the amazing grace and forgiveness offered to us?

 PRAYER FOCUS

Thank God for His wonderful forgiveness, and ask the Lord to give you the grace to forgive others.

 ASSIGNMENT

Read Chapter 2, "Expect Joy." Contemplate your own experience of the "joy of the Lord." Is it real in your life? Why or why not?

_____
_____
_____
_____
_____
_____
_____
_____
_____
_____
_____
_____

LESSON 2
EXPECT JOY

LESSON TOPIC

The kind of joy we can expect as members of God's family.

FELLOWSHIP PRIMER

Ask the class to distinguish between "joy" and "happiness." Make two columns on a chalkboard or overhead, and list the characteristics of each.

KEY QUESTIONS

1. How does the story in Acts 3 relate to the fact that we can "expect joy" in our walk with the Lord (i.e., what is the spiritual application)?
2. What is a key prerequisite before we can experience the joy of Jesus?
3. What does it mean to have a "new standing" with God?
4. Why is "happiness" short-lived whereas joy can be for the long haul?
5. What's the difference between having joy in a circumstance versus joy for a circumstance?
6. The counterfeit version of joy offered by the world lacks two qualities. What are they?

7. Why would it be impossible to develop a "standard" for a joyful demeanor?

8. Is it enough to just experience the joy of the Lord for ourselves, or is there something we should do about it?

PRAYER FOCUS

Confess any sin that may be blocking the joy of Jesus in your life. Thank God for the reality of His joy even in the midst of difficult circumstances. Ask the Lord to enable you to spread joy to others wherever you go.

ASSIGNMENT

Read Chapter 3, "Expect Peace" and Mark 4:35-41. Write your own definition of "the peace of God."

_____

_____

_____

_____

_____

_____

_____

_____

_____

_____

_____

LESSON 3
EXPECT PEACE

LESSON TOPIC

How we can expect and experience the peace of God in the daily walk.

FELLOWSHIP PRIMER

Ask for testimonies from the group about times when they have experienced the peace of God.

KEY QUESTIONS

1. In Mark 4:35-41, why were the disciples so angry with Christ?
2. We can have God's peace because of what?
3. What kinds of things would "the peace of the world" be based upon?
4. Was Paul "brave" or "stupid" to tell his shipmates to "keep up their courage" in Acts 27? Why?
5. How does Philippians 4:11-13 apply to the situations you are facing in your life right now?
6. What's the difference between a "peacemaker" and a "peacekeeper," and why is this an important distinction?
7. How can we "maintain the peace" in our daily walk with God?

8. How can God's peace become our "umpire" in all circumstances?

PRAYER FOCUS

Thank God for the peace you can have through the cross work of His Son. Ask the Lord to make you a real "peacemaker" in all the areas of your life.

ASSIGNMENT

Read Chapter 4, "Expect Trials." Can you relate personally to the opening illustration about Jim and Rhoda, or do you know of someone else who can?

_____

_____

_____

_____

_____

_____

_____

_____

_____

_____

_____

_____

_____

_____

LESSON 4
EXPECT TRIALS

LESSON TOPIC

Why we can expect trials, but also expect special strength from God to get through them.

FELLOWSHIP PRIMER

Ask one or two in the group to share a story about an unexpected trial that came into their lives. How did they feel about it? What were the questions that they wanted to ask?

KEY QUESTIONS

1. Why is it that some people seem to experience more than their "fair share" of trials?
2. What are the three things that can bring about trials in our lives?
3. What do Adam and Eve have to do with the trials we experience?
4. In what sense can we sometimes say, "God gave me this hardship"? What are some biblical illustrations of this?
5. What part does "human error" play in our experience of difficulty?
6. What is the ultimate purpose of our trials?

7. "Hardship will either make us bitter or better." What does this mean?

8. If we do not "feel" God's presence in the midst of our trials, does that mean He is far from us or we have committed sin?

PRAYER FOCUS

Ask God to show you how He is using those trials in your life right now to make you more like Jesus. Thank Him for His strength to carry on during troubled times.

ASSIGNMENT

Read Chapter 5, "Expect Temptation." Consider your own life: what is your greatest temptation?

_____

_____

_____

_____

_____

_____

_____

_____

_____

_____

_____

_____

LESSON 5
EXPECT TEMPTATION

LESSON TOPIC

The nature of the temptation we can expect to come our way, and the steps to victory over it.

FELLOWSHIP PRIMER

As a class, discuss the shocking true story in the introduction about the pastor who was robbing banks to pay for his sexual addiction. Then ask, "Do each of us have the potential for this kind of evil?"

KEY QUESTIONS

1. How do we know that temptation is "common to man" apart from what Scripture teaches?
2. Why would Satan want to make us feel "alone" in our temptation?
3. What is the difference between trials and temptations?
4. Why is it important not to view God as a source of temptation?
5. What are the three sources of temptation in our lives?
6. Why are monks in a monastery not immune from temptation?
7. What is the devil's approach to us in temptation?

8. Discuss the "sin cycle" and its implications. How can the cycle be broken?

PRAYER FOCUS

Ask God to show you any areas in which you have allowed yourself to get into tempting scenarios. Pray for His power to overcome the world, the flesh and the devil.

ASSIGNMENT

Read Chapter 6, "Expect Persecution." Think about those times when you have been persecuted for Christ's sake.

_____

_____

_____

_____

_____

_____

_____

_____

_____

_____

_____

_____

_____

_____

_____

LESSON 6
EXPECT PERSECUTION

LESSON TOPIC

Why we should expect persecution and how we should respond to it.

FELLOWSHIP PRIMER

Encourage class members to discuss their personal experiences of persecution—regardless of how minor it may have been. What was their reaction to this? Was it surprising to be ridiculed for their faith?

KEY QUESTIONS

1. What was the key distinction between the "persecution" of Pastor A and Pastor B in the opening illustration?
2. What are the three reasons we encounter persecution, according to the book?
3. What is "guilt by association" as it relates to our Christianity?
4. Can we be persecuted for simply telling the truth?
5. What's so offensive about a "godly lifestyle" to some people?
6. What three things should characterize our response to persecution? Discuss the implications of each one.

7. What "good company" are we in by suffering for Christ?

8. How can we have the ability to respond with love for our persecutors?

PRAYER FOCUS

Ask God to give you His grace in the midst of persecution. Ask Him and then believe Him to love the perpetrators of your suffering through you.

ASSIGNMENT

Read Chapter 7, "Expect Doubts." Think about what issues have caused you to doubt in your Christian life.

_____

_____

_____

_____

_____

_____

_____

_____

_____

_____

_____

_____

_____

LESSON 7
EXPECT DOUBTS

LESSON TOPIC

Why we can expect doubts to come our way, but also expect that faith will ultimately win.

FELLOWSHIP PRIMER

Invite the group to share some of their own struggles with the issue of doubting in the Christian life.

KEY QUESTIONS

1. Can you relate to the periods of doubt in the lives of "Missionary Jim," Elijah and John the Baptist? Why or why not?
2. What are four things that can lead to doubt, according to the book?
3. Why is it important to understand the "frailty of the flesh"?
4. "He is as crafty as he is cruel." What is this saying about Satan?
5. Why does unconfessed sin in our lives create doubt?
6. Is Christianity something that can be "proved" using the "scientific method"? Why is it important to understand the implications of this?

7. What is the best way back to faith when we've been trapped by doubt?
8. What role does a daily devotional time play in alleviating our doubts?

PRAYER FOCUS

Thank the Lord for the fact that He understands our periods of doubt. Ask Him to help you work through your doubts utilizing the disciplines of studying His Word and prayer.

ASSIGNMENT

Read Chapter 8, "Expect Growth." Consider the growth you've experienced in your walk with the Lord.

_____
_____
_____
_____
_____
_____
_____
_____
_____
_____
_____
_____
_____

LESSON 8
EXPECT GROWTH

LESSON TOPIC

How God leads us on the pathway to a growing, fulfilling relationship with Christ.

FELLOWSHIP PRIMER

Using a chalkboard or overhead projector, ask the group to list things that help Christians grow in their walk with the Lord. Make sure that the list includes the subjects of the past four chapters (trials, persecutions, temptations and doubts).

KEY QUESTIONS

1. How did the opening illustration about the author's daughter bring together the elements of the four previous chapters?
2. Why might we call Jacob's home a "dysfunctional family"?
3. What was the ultimate sign of Joseph's growth through his incredible trials?
4. What do you think was Paul's "thorn in the flesh" and why?
5. How is growth experienced through the process of temptation?
6. Can we grow even if we yield to temptation?

7. What was the evidence that Stephen had grown through his ordeals of persecution?

8. What four things does the author say we can do to enhance our own spiritual growth? Discuss the implications of each one.

PRAYER FOCUS

Ask God to keep you on the cutting edge of spiritual growth in your daily walk.

ASSIGNMENT

Read Chapter 9, "Expect Gifts." What do you think your spiritual gift(s) might be?

_____

_____

_____

_____

_____

_____

_____

_____

_____

_____

_____

_____

_____

_____

_____

LESSON 9
EXPECT GIFTS

LESSON TOPIC

The importance of understanding, discovering and using our spiritual gift(s) for the building of Christ's kingdom.

FELLOWSHIP PRIMER

Ask group members to briefly describe their favorite Christmas present from their childhood, and what made it so special.

KEY QUESTIONS

1. How are the "gifts of the Spirit" similar in nature to the gifts we give to each other at Christmas?
2. How can we be sure that every Christian will receive at least one spiritual gift?
3. What is a "supernatural ability"?
4. How should those with fewer gifts be treated in the body of Christ? Why?
5. Can we all expect to have the same spiritual gift? Why or why not?
6. What are the implications of the fact that the Holy Spirit selects our spiritual gifts for us?
7. What is the bottom-line purpose of our spiritual gift(s)?

8. How can we discover our spiritual gift(s)?
9. Why is it so crucial to seek the Giver rather than His gifts?

PRAYER FOCUS

Thank God for the fact that you can expect spiritual gifts. Ask Him to clearly reveal to you which gift(s) you have, and then ask Him to give you the strength and wisdom to use them for His glory.

ASSIGNMENT

Read Chapter 10, "Expect Service." Have you found your place of service in the body of Christ?

_____

_____

_____

_____

_____

_____

_____

_____

_____

_____

_____

_____

_____

_____

_____

LESSON 10
EXPECT SERVICE

LESSON FOCUS

We should expect service as a natural response of gratitude to God for all that He has done for us.

FELLOWSHIP PRIMER

Ask the group what Peter's mother-in-law did after she was healed. What does that say to us?

KEY QUESTIONS

1. How do we sometimes take advantage of God's great grace?
2. How does a distorted view of God keep us from seeing our need to serve Him fully?
3. "We do not serve the Savior to earn our salvation, but we serve Him because He saved us!" What is the meaning of this statement?
4. What is "a faith that works"?
5. Who is called "to do the work of the ministry," and why?
6. What are the three roadblocks to servanthood mentioned in the book? Discuss their implications.
7. How can we "get started" in serving the Lord?

8. Why is serving the Lord not always "easy" and yet "fulfilling"?

PRAYER FOCUS

Ask God to show you the specific place of service that He has for you in the body of Christ. Trust Him for the time, gifts and energy to work for Him.

ASSIGNMENT

Read Chapter 11, "Expect Accountability." Would you say that you have enough accountability in your Christian life at the present time?

_____

_____

_____

_____

_____

_____

_____

_____

_____

_____

_____

_____

_____

_____

_____

_____

_____

LESSON 11
EXPECT ACCOUNTABILITY

LESSON TOPIC

The importance of three-way accountability: to God, to the body of Christ and to an individual or small group.

FELLOWSHIP PRIMER

Ask the class members to describe and discuss the accountability relationships they have where they work. How important is accountability in the workplace? How is accountability in one's spiritual life similar—and different?

KEY QUESTIONS

1. In what ways are we accountable to God?
2. What can keep us from being frightened at the prospect of standing before a holy God?
3. Why is it so critical to keep "current accounts" with God on a daily basis?
4. If the church is far from perfect, why should we be accountable to the body of Christ?
5. For what two things, according to the book, are we accountable to the church?
6. What is the third level of accountability and why is it important, too?

7. What are some dangers to avoid as we look for an individual or small group to confide in?

8. Who is the "ultimate prayer partner" and what is His role?

PRAYER FOCUS

Pray that God will help you to live your life in the light of this three-fold accountability. Ask God to clearly show you that friend or small group with whom you can share your struggles.

ASSIGNMENT

Read Chapter 12, "Expect Victory."

LESSON 12
EXPECT VICTORY

LESSON TOPIC

How to attain the victorious, Spirit-filled Christian life.

FELLOWSHIP PRIMER

Ask the class to discuss the meaning of Ephesians 5:18. How does someone who is drunk compare to someone who is "filled with the Spirit"?

KEY QUESTIONS

1. What did you think of the chapter's opening story of the millionaire buying the poor man's property? Discuss its implications.
2. What are some of the things that reveal our inadequacy to live a successful Christian life in our own strength?
3. What is the process of "reckoning"? What does it mean to be "dead and alive" at the same time?
4. In looking over the contrasting lists of characteristics from the carnal nature and the Christ nature, where do you see yourself? Which nature is really in control?
5. How do we know that it's "carnal" to gossip?

6. How does anger fit into the Spirit-filled life? (Read Acts 13:6-12.)
7. What does the author mean by "a crisis followed by a daily process"? Why is this necessary?
8. What should a Spirit-filled Christian do if he or she sins?

PRAYER FOCUS

If you have never asked the Holy Spirit to fill you, do so now. As you reckon yourself dead to sin and alive to the Savior, He will do this! Thank Him for doing what He promised!

ASSIGNMENT

Read Chapter 13, Expect Eternal Life, and the epilogue, What Not to Expect.

LESSON 13
EXPECT ETERNAL LIFE
AND
WHAT NOT TO EXPECT

LESSON FOCUS

What to expect hereafter and what not to expect here.

FELLOWSHIP PRIMER

Ask the class to discuss their vision of what heaven will be like. How would they describe it? What will it look like? What will our new bodies look like? Allow a very open-ended discussion.

KEY QUESTIONS

1. What experiences can bring the concept of eternal life closer to home for us? Why?
2. How is it that we can expect eternal life now?
3. What does it mean to be "asleep" according to the apostle Paul?
4. What will be the order of events at Christ's second coming?
5. What will be the most glorious aspect of our new bodies?
6. What is the "double blessing" alluded to in First Thessalonians 4:17?

7. Why is the word "sea" significant in Revelation 21:1, in reference to what heaven will be like?

8. What four things does the author tell us we should *not* expect while still here on this earth? How should a Christian deal with these issues?

PRAYER FOCUS

Thank God for the wonderful, indescribable things that lie ahead! Ask Him to make you effective in outreach so that others can join us in our eternal home.

OTHER BOOKS BY TOM ALLEN

I Wish You Could Meet My Mom and Dad

Rock 'n Roll, the Bible, and the Mind

Congregations in Conflict

*Ten Foolish Things Christians
Do to Stunt Their Growth*

Joy Comes in the Mourning
(by David Johnson with Tom Allen)

A Closer Look at Dr. Laura

With No Remorse

Leading the Followers by Following the Leader
(by Dennis Gorton with Tom Allen)

BOOKLETS BY TOM ALLEN

Spiritual Leadership Begins at Home

Let Him that Is without Sin . . .

Hope for Hurting Parents